Thick as a Brick

A musical

John Godber

Samuel French — London
www.samuelfrench-london.co.uk

ISBN 0 573 08127 1

THICK AS A BRICK

First performed by the Hull Truck Theatre Company in April 1999, with the following cast of characters.

Mary Clifford	Gilly Tompkins
Jimmy Naylor/Colin Grey/Gary Fox	Gordon Kane
Tom/Headmaster/Ronnie Baines	Dicken Ashworth
Stacey Naylor	Lyanne Compton
Kerry Shields	Jo Theaker
Maggie Brooke	Sally Carman

Music by John Pattison
Additional lyrics by Jane Thornton
Directed by John Godber
Choreography by Lucy Cullingford

CHARACTERS

Mary Clifford, 42. A nervous type. She is an ex-teacher who is returning to education after a fifteen year lay off. She is extremely bright with a Ph.D. in Romantic drama, but has the affliction of a slight stammer.

Tom Duncan, 50. Has been in education for as long as he can remember. Despite being tired and jaundiced he does try his best to save a sinking ship. He is longing, however, for his place in the sun. His place is Tuscany, where he dreams of buying a holiday home.

Gary Fox, 38. The PE teacher at Common Road. He is sharp and angular. Nasty and hard-faced.

Stacey Naylor, 16. An attractive but difficult child. She is not of high academic ability but is street wise and savvy. She has a natural ability at dance and drama.

Kerry Shields, 16. A shy and quiet girl. She is a real dreamer but her birdlike qualities give the impression of someone not always focused.

Maggie Brooke, 16. Truculent and dour. She is uninterested in anything at all, and is very much a passenger in the trio.

Jimmy Naylor, 45. Stacey's father. He is a bright and worldly but uneducated man. He has been in and out of prison several times, and is aggressive and frightening. His wife died five years ago. He is extremely protective of Stacey.

Ronny Baines, 50. Runs the Astoria Guest House, near King's Cross. It is part brothel part hotel, indeed Ronny is part landlord and part pimp.

The action of the play takes place in a fictional East Yorkshire secondary school

The time—the present

PRODUCTION NOTES

The Place

Common Road High School: a failing school with a high truancy rate and the dubious honour of being bottom of the National league tables twice!

The Set

Essentially an open space which will have to accommodate a number of different locations. Since the play is about imagination, the set should mirror this. Only chairs and tables will be used, though a number of other indicators should be used for the Marina and the Astoria Hotel.

Doubling

The opening Prologue involves everyone save Mary. The actors playing the students take part in the opening scene. Jimmy doubles with Gary. Tom also doubles with Seedy Ronny.

MUSICAL NUMBERS

ACT I

Playover: children shouting and playing

The Lights fade to black. Music

Five actors enter. Tom, Gary, and three female teachers, June, Joyce and Lynne

A musical routine-which incorporates strong movements depicting teacher frustation, is played out on stage. The actors suddenly stop. As each actor speaks they are spotlit by a vertical spotlight until all five are lit

Overture: I Shalln't Say It Again

Tom	I shalln't say it again!
Lynn	I shalln't say it again!
Joyce	I shalln't say it again!
June	I shalln't say it again!
Gary	I shalln't say it again!
All	I shalln't say it again!

From here all the actors speak the verse in choric fashion, though they still retain individual intonations

Tom	Right, shut up!
	I said, shut up!
	I didn't say chatter
	I said, shut up!
	And take off your coats!
	And shift your bags!
	And look this way.
	And lose the fags!
Lynn	Right, sit down!
	I said, sit down!

I didn't say slouch,
Or fool around.
Come off that table!
Come off that shelf!
Come off those wires!
You'll kill yourself

Tom   I shalln't say it again!
Lynn   I shalln't say it again!
Joyce   I shalln't say it again!
June   I shalln't say it again.
Gary   I shalln't say it again.
All   I shalln't say it again!

Joyce   Right, look this way!
I said, look this way!
I didn't say chew!
I didn't say play!
I said, look this way!
I said, look this way!
How many times do I have to say?

June   Will everybody look this way?
Will you look this way?
Do you think you could?
Am I doing this for my own good?
Put down your bags
Open your books!
And don't give me those dirty looks.
I said…

Tom   I shalln't say it again!
Lynn   I shalln't say it again!
Joyce   I shalln't say it again!
June   I shalln't say it again.
Gary   I shalln't say it again!
All   I shalln't say it again!

Gary   Why does it have to be a drain?
Every lesson is just the same.
What do you think it is,
All   A game?
June & Lynn & Joyce What's happening here is causing strife!

Tom & Gary Waken up you sods,
                    This is your life!
June & Lynn & Joyce It's your lucky chance.
All   Your lucky day.

Tom   I shalln't say it again!
Lynn   I shalln't say it again!
Joyce   I shalln't say it again!
June   I shalln't say it again!
Gary   I shalln't say it again!
All   I shalln't say it again!

                 So will everybody look this way?
Tom   Will everybody look this way?
Lynn   Will everybody look this way!
Joyce   Will everybody look this way!
June   Will everybody look this way!
Gary   Will everybody look this way!
All   Will everybody please look this way!
    (*Quietly*) Thank you!

SCENE 1

Staff room morning meeting

Tom addresses the throng, holding a number of note cards. June, Joyce, Lynn and Gary sit and perch or read their papers. They are listening to the morning's briefing

Tom Morning everyone. Sorry we're a bit pushed this morning, but you know how it is, etc.! Staff off, etc.! I suppose you've all seen this morning's *Telegraph* or whatever! The league tables are in there, and for anyone who wants to make themselves ill you'll see Common Road High School in a strong position, tucked well in at the bottom, etc. Holding up everyone else! A few things before we get at them... (*He reads from his cards*) Number one: Just to alert everyone that Stacey Naylor is back in school again! So if you wonder what she's doing, you'll be pleased to know that we've got her back.

A number of staff groan

Secondly: Tony Watson, can we ensure that he sits near the front, he can't hear on his left side apparently, so turn him sideways or whatever, etc.! And just to say Foxy's basketball team are through to the third round, well done to them! And can I thank all those who attended Ron Baker's funeral at the weekend. Not a pleasant occasion at the best of times! I know that Martine, his partner, was much comforted by those expressions of regret, so many thanks! Ron's classes will be covered by a supply lady for the rest of this term, if she appears: though I think there's been an accident on the road in etc. so … anyway! Oh, the cover sheet is up by the way so…

A huge groan from the rest of the staff as they move up stage. Tom puts away his reference cards. He hates staff meetings, it is a relief when they're over. As Lynn moves to exit she calls to Tom

Lynn Do you know what's happening with room five-oh-five?
Tom I'm on to them!

Gary collects his papers

Gary Tom, balls!
Tom Thanks, Foxy!
Gary We need to talk.
Lynn I think it's still raining in.
Tom I've been on to them six times this morning. I'll give them another ring. Are you short of buckets?
Lynn I've got more buckets than kids in there at the moment!

Gary exits with Lynn

Mary Clifford arrives. She is flustered and lost. She is bright with glasses. Fairly modern but not trendy

Mary Sorry. Mr Duncan?
Tom Ah!
Mary Mary Clifford. S-sorry, I'm la-ate.
Tom Sad news about Ron Baker, but there you are…
Mary Is he the teacher I'm covering for?
Tom Heart attack!
Mary Oh dear!
Tom Prime of his life!
Mary Oh dear.
Tom Stress, they reckoned!
Mary Oh dear!
Tom Only forty-five.

Mary Oh dear!

Tom I told the Chair of Education that he'd be sorely missed. A one man workhorse! So do you know much about Common Road?

Mary Well, no, but I'm a fast study!

Tom You'll need to be! Do you live locally?

Mary Goole at the moment, but everything could change.

Tom Some people travel from Leeds, God knows what for. You would have thought they could find somewhere equally awful on their own patch.

Mary Oh well...

Tom I'm joking! I have a queer sense of humour, Mrs Clifford. You'll soon come to realize that!

Mary Oh right!

Tom I have a sardonic sense of humour. My wife calls it gallows humour. And the sooner they bring them back the better. That's what Polly says. I tell her to shut up and put the kettle on. We have to laugh here, Mrs Clifford, we're bottom of the league. Twice in a row, now that is an achievement! I'm only joking. No, I'm not really, but there you go. So what was the school like you taught in?

Mary It was fifteen years ago!

Tom Well, I suppose we're lucky you can recognize a school.

Mary It was an E.P.A. School in a mining area.

Tom You'll know all about tough kids, then?

Mary Well, they can't have changed that much.

Tom Got their heads stuck in a computer screen most of the time, watching some filth, lucky sods, eh? Still, we mustn't grumble.

Mary Small victories!

Tom Ron Baker had a saying about this school, "You must live every day here like it's going to be your last, because one day you're going to be right".

Mary Sounds a little bit gr-grim!

Tom Give a dog a bad name!

Mary It's about drops in the ocean, isn't it?

Tom Absolutely! You've got a timetable I take it?

Mary Yes, the lady at the office...

Tom Mavis! She runs the school really, when she goes we've all had it. You've got a map, have you? I'd take you around myself but I've got a leak.

Gary Fox enters the staff room. He is laden with files and books. He also has a basket-ball

Gary Balls!

Tom This is the supply woman! (*He introduces Mary*)

Gary shakes her hand

Gary Gary Fox.

Tom Head of PE. He's after new balls.

Gary Barry Folds, truancy again!

Tom See Brian!

Gary Brian's off.

Tom If Maureen's here ask her to see to it, I'm up to my neck! Lynn Webster's got a drip in five-oh-five. And it's not one of the kids. (*To Mary*) Gary'll take you down there.

Tom exits

Gary and Mary are left together. Silence

Gary You're covering for Baker, then?

Mary Just for a term.

Gary He's got all the dregs. When they brought in the National Curriculum, drama went out to the fringes. All that poncy stuff got pushed to the sidelines. They reckon that's why he had the heart attack, all that effort and little reward. I reckon it was the performance-related pay myself.

Mary Really?

Gary Well, he wouldn't benefit from it, would he?

Gary and Mary turn suddenly and simulate walking

Listen, as long as they can read and write and don't cause any trouble on the way home, parents around here aren't generally bothered! We've got the largest teenage pregnancy rate in the area, and we're third in the truancy tables. Apart from basketball it's what the kids around here do the best!

Mary Oh, it's all coming b-back.

Gary What is?

Mary Why I left teaching in the f-f-first place!

Music. The Lights fade

SCENE 2

Drama studio

Music fades

Mary and Gary have arrived at the drama studio

Three girls have entered. Stacey, a tough looking and mature girl, wearing hardly any school uniform and a too short mini skirt, sits with Kerry, a smaller and skinnier girl, also wearing very little uniform. They lounge on a number of chairs. Maggie, a larger and sullen girl, sits nearby, listening to her headphones. All three girls are sixteen, bored and ready to leave

Gary attempts to get their attention. Mary stands by apprehensively

Gary Morning! Is this Mr Baker's class?

No reply from the girls

   Is this all there is?

No reply from the girls

   Can we just take the register before we push on?

He reads from the class register

   Barry Adams? Peter Armley? Saul Bellman? No? Not here? How about Mark Goodman?
Kerry (*whispering*) Left.
Gary Sorry?
Kerry Left.
Gary Left? How can he have left, you should be here till July.
Maggie Well, he has!
Gary What about Shaun Hepton?
Kerry He never comes to this lesson.
Gary Sam Roberts?
Kerry Got shits!
Gary Right! Who are you, then?
Kerry Kerry Shields!
Gary OK, and the next one?
Maggie Mag.
Gary Mag what?
Maggie Maggie!
Gary Maggie what?
Maggie Maggie Brooke.
Gary Margaret Brooke.
Maggie Not Margaret, Maggie!
Gary Whatever. And the next one?
Kerry That's Stacey Naylor.
Gary OK. This is Mrs Clifford. She's going to be taking Mr Baker's classes.

So I want you to be as good for her as you were for him. (*To Mary*) I'll leave
you to it, then!

Gary exits

Mary stands looking at the girls. Silence

Mary Ca-can yo-you all come around here, then?

A beat

Stacey Have you heard her?
Mary Br-bring a se-seat and let's h-have a c-chat, shall we?
Stacey A ch-chat? Ch-chat ch-chat?

The girls laugh at Mary

Mary Br-bring a seat!
Stacey That's why she didn't do the register, we'd have been here all day!

Kerry and Maggie find this funny

Mary Co-come on, let's just have a natter.
Maggie We don't want to natter.
Mary I'll come to you, then, sh-shall l?
Maggie Oh God!

*Mary picks up a chair and walks over to the group. She sits on the chair as
Maggie rises and sullenly walks across the drama studio and sits elsewhere*

Mary Aren't you joining us?
Maggie No.

*Stacey and Kerry take their seats and move elsewhere in the room. Mary
leaves her seat and walks over to their new position*

Mary So what kind of things have you been doing lately?
Kerry Our projects.
Mary And what are they?
Kerry We have to make a play up for GCSE.
Maggie Yes. We just sit and chat.
Mary So what is the play about?
Maggie Is there going to be a World War?

Mary Can we just concentrate on this?
Maggie If there is I'm flitting!
Stacey Where to, you dildo!
Mary I wonder if you'd mind just pa-paying attention. And having a chat first so I can get to know you?
Kerry Miss, we want to do our project.
Maggie Oh God!

The girls reluctantly give some attention

Mary So what sort of things are you interested in?
Stacey Do one, love, will you?
Mary Are there any things that interest you?
Stacey What, apart from Robbie?
Mary Robbie?
Stacey Don't you know who Robbie is?
Mary He's a singer?
Stacey Oh God!
Maggie Robbie's crap!
Stacey Not.
Maggie Snot!
Stacey Not.
Mary OK, what kind of things in school are you interested in?
Stacey Karl Evans.
Maggie Yes!
Mary So are you interested in anything out of school.
Maggie Karl Evans!
Stacey Not!
Maggie Snot!
Stacey Not!

Mary decides on a different angle

Mary So you're not interested in anything in sc-school?
Stacey God!
Mary Did you do drama in the other school you went to?
Stacey Which one?

There is much laughter from the girls

Mary OK! So let's do a little bit of an exercise, shall we?
Maggie No.
Mary We'll do a word association game. Don't worry, it won't kill you.

Maggie (*mimicking*) It mi-might!

More laughing from the trio

Mary I'll say a word and you say the first thing that comes in your head, OK?
Stacey Oh no!
Mary No, I haven't started yet!

The girls laugh beyond the call of duty

Stacey Oh, I thought you'd started.
Mary No, not yet, I'll say I've started when I start, right?
Stacey Left.

The girls laugh once more

Mary No, hang on.
Kerry Hang out.
Maggie We've done this, it's crap.
Kerry I haven't!
Mary Well, let's have a go at doing it again and I'll see how crap you are.
Maggie I'm not crap, it's the game what's crap!

A beat

Mary OK, here goes! Apple.
Stacey Apple!
Kerry Apple!
Maggie Apple!
Mary No, yo-you have to say the word that you associate with apple. Not say what I said. So like, if I said black, you might say white.
Kerry I might say grey.
Mary You might.
Kerry I might say night.
Mary That would be good.
Stacey Doesn't rhyme though!
Mary OK. Here we go, ready?
Stacey Steady.
Maggie Eddie.
Kerry Izzard.
Mary Eh?
Stacey What?
Maggie Who?

Kerry You?
Stacey Me?
Maggie Pee!
Kerry Me?
Stacey You.
Maggie Poo!
Mary Shoe!
Stacey Arsehole!

The girls break into laughter

Mary OK, OK, you're too good for me, let's move on to something else. I
don't think it's going to work with so few of us. What about music, what
kind of music are you interested in?
Maggie Good music!
Mary So what about dance, are you interested in dance?
Maggie Can't we just sit and chat?
Mary (*to Stacey*) What do you do?
Stacey Why, me?
Mary Do you dance?
Stacey Why, are you asking?

Laughter from the trio

Maggie Oh, kinky!
Stacey Yes, I'm a stripper in a club.
Mary Oh, really?
Maggie No, O'Reilly's!

More laughter from the trio

Stacey Not.
Maggie Snot!
Kerry Not!
Stacey Snot!
Maggie Not!
Stacey Snot!
Maggie Big not!
Stacey Big snot!
Mary You think that's good, do you?
Stacey Ye-yes, we d-do! M-Miss!
Mary Oh, here we go! The same old st-stuff!
Stacey Ooohhh!

Mary Why are you doing that? You don't know what you're dealing with, do you? I might be anybody, I might be dangerous. I might be totally unhinged. But because I'm in a classroom you think you can just mess me about! And the staff can't even touch you, now can they? Look at you, I used to eat kids like you for my breakfast, all right, sk-skinny?

Kerry Yes, Miss.

Mary All right, grunter?

Maggie Uh.

Mary So, let's find a space, shall we?

The trio slowly get to their feet

Look at you, what's wrong with you?

Music. The Lights change as the girls start to move to the music

Song 1: Bored

Girls	We're so bored
	We're bored,
Kerry	Every syllable we hear just makes us snore
Maggie	She's dull
All	She's thick,
Stacey	Her boffin talk just makes us
Stacey & Maggie	Want to sick
Kerry	It's
All	rubbish
Maggie	It's all
All	Pap
Kerry	What she makes us do is
Maggie	Just a
Stacey	Just a
Kerry	Just a load of
All	Crap!

Stacey	She's like them all!
Kerry & Maggie	They think they're gods
Stacey	But they're not
All	They all boring educated sods!

Kerry & Maggie Doo doo doo, doo doo doo doo doo
Kerry & Stacey We're so bored doo doo doo doo doo
Kerry & Maggie Doo doo doo, doo doo doo doo doo

Kerry & Stacey We're so bored doo doo doo doo doo

Maggie	They're not like us, they think they are
Kerry	Who are they, then?
Maggie & Stacey	They roll around in their shiny, shiny newly plated cars
Kerry	Our cars are wrecks
Maggie & Stacey	They stand on bricks
Kerry	The engine and the sump
All	We've still to fix.

We're so bored we're bored so stiff.

Kerry & Stacey	Why don't she take a running jump
Maggie	Right off-f-f-f-f-f
All	A cliff?

Maggie	Get out our face!
Kerry & Stacey	Stop harping on
Maggie	We know it's just a
Kerry & Stacey	Job that must be done!
Maggie	So what's the fuss?
Kerry & Stacey	So why all this
Maggie	The more she gets red-faced
Kerry & Stacey	The more we take the piss…
Kerry	Miss!
Maggie	Miss!
Stacey	Miss!
All	We're so bored, we get so bored
Kerry & Maggie	We really can't be bothered
Kerry & Maggie & Stacey	If we're left and get ignored
All	We're so bored, we're bored so stiff
Kerry & Stacey	Why don't she take a running jump
Maggie	Right off-f-f-f-f-f
All	A cliff

Maggie	Do you think she'll cope?
	Do you think she'll last the course?
	(Speaking) I doubt it
Maggie & Stacey	We'll make her shout and moan until she's hoarse.

Kerry	We know the form.
Maggie & Stacey	We know the game.
Kerry	We know they try the chatty stuff,
All	They're all the same.

Maggie   She'll not last long,
Kerry & Stacey Maybe a week.
Maggie   Then the Head will
Kerry & Stacey Send another gormless geek.
Maggie   We've seen them off!
Kerry & Stacey We wear them out…
Maggie   In twenty minutes' time
Kerry & Stacey She'll scream and shout.

All   She'll tear out her hair.
                Run off in tears
                We're the kind of class that every teacher fears.
                We're so bored
                We're bored so stiff
                That's why we're bored.
                Why can't she take a running jump right off-f-f-f-f-f a cliff!

Stacey   That's why we're bored.
Others   Doo doo doo, doo doo doo doo doo
                Just leave us be.
                Doo doo doo, doo doo doo doo doo
                Just leave us be
                Doo doo doo, doo doo doo doo doo
                Just leave us.
                Doo doo doo, doo doo doo
                Bored!

At the end of the song the girls end up seated as they were at the beginning of the song

Music stops. The Lights return to the previous state. A loud school bell rings. The sounds of children shouting and screaming is heard. In the original a taped musical sting linked this scene. Alternatively, sound cues of general school noise could also work

The girls place the chairs in a format that represents the staff room and run off

SCENE 3

Drama studio. Night

Music fades

Mary is organizing some of her papers in her briefcase

As Tom wanders in he looks more hassled than previously

Tom Six days for the roof to be fixed! Six days! The Lord made the world in six days and we can't get the roof fixed. Still here, then?
Mary Just about!
Tom I remember my first term. Battle scars, three scalps. Five dead! I don't know what I expected but whatever it was they hadn't trained me for it. I jest of course!
Mary Yes, right!
Tom Sorry I haven't been in much this last fortnight, but we've got another Ofsted. Staying late?
Mary I was, I put a notice up for another dance class. Thought I'd try and get them motivated, but? I had two last week but it doesn't look like they're coming back! So I'll go home and make myself a pot noodle or something.
Tom Oh, well, you have to start somewhere. From little acorns etc.
Mary That's right.
Tom Keep at them. Good-night!

Tom exits

Mary Good-night! (*She sits*)

Music underscores

   Stacey, Maggie and Kerry sheepishly enter

Stacey Is this the dance thing?
Mary It might be!
Stacey Came to see what was going on!
Mary Nothing at the moment, I'm about to go home.
Maggie I wanted to go home and all but it's pissing it down.
Mary So you've only come because it's raining? Well, go away! I don't want you. You either come because you're interested or you can leg it.
Maggie Leg it? Have you heard her? You're supposed to be a bloody teacher!
Stacey You teach dance, then?
Mary Amongst other things!
Stacey What sort of dance is it?
Mary What sort do you want it to be?
Stacey Is it disco?
Mary Why don't you come and sit down and we'll have a ch-chat!
Kerry Miss, can I leave me coat on?
Maggie I didn't want to come, me.
Mary Change the record, mate!

Maggie Eh?

Mary You've told me that!

Maggie I think you're a bogey. From up my nose.

Mary Yes, I am.

Kerry Miss, can I leave my coat on?

Mary Do you think you'll be able to dance with your coat on?

Kerry No.

Mary Well, then.

A pause

Kerry Miss, can I leave my coat on!

Mary What are you like? You're about five, aren't you? Miss, can I leave me coat on?

The girls laugh

Kerry Miss, I'm cold!

Maggie Can't do much dancing with just three! You can dance and I'll watch. (*She plonks herself in a chair*)

Stacey You go clubbing, then, miss?

Mary I'm out every night.

Maggie Not!

Mary Snot!

Maggie What?

Mary Don't you believe me?

Stacey No.

Mary Why not?

Stacey Because teachers are boring!

Mary Yes, that's why they become teachers.

Kerry Is it?

Mary You have to be boring to be a teacher in the first place.

Maggie Yes, I've heard that!

Mary There's a special college you have to go to!

Kerry Are you married, miss?

Mary I am at the moment!

Stacey Are you going to show us how to dance, then, miss?

Mary Yes, I'll prance about, so you can have a good laugh, shall I?

Stacey Yes, brilliant!

Maggie Yes, come on!

Mary OK. I'll move about a bit. Just to get warmed up, but if any of you laugh, you have to get up, OK?

Stacey Yes, all right!

A beat

Mary It may be a bit seventies, but…!

Kerry Miss, can I keep my coat on?

Mary Oh, shut up, you silly arse! (*She clicks on some music*) Wait for it! Here we go! (*She plays a track on the cassette and begins to move to it. She knows it is embarrassing but goes for it*)

The kids find it funny. She is genuinely funny

Right, you laughed and you laughed! Come on, up you get!

Maggie I didn't laugh, I was just smirking!

Mary Everybody who laughed, on their feet! Let's see if you can do any better! Kerry!

Kerry Oh, miss!

Mary Let's see if you can do any better.

Kerry No, miss, I can't, I've got my coat on!

Mary Oh, yeah, very good!

Kerry Well, I have!

Mary Maggie, come on!

Maggie I didn't laugh!

Mary Stacey?

Stacey No.

Mary Come on, you laughed!

Stacey No way.

Mary Come on, don't think you can get away with it! You laughed, I saw you.

Stacey I don't fancy it.

Kerry Come on, Stacey, you do it, she's brilliant, miss!

Stacey slowly stirs

Stacey OK, st-stand back, miss!

Mary Oh, right, then!

Kerry Miss, she's brilliant.

Stacey OK, don't try this at home, right! (*She takes centre stage. She starts to dance*)

Jimmy Naylor, an aggressive man in his mid-forties enters. He turns off the cassette

Silence

Jimmy What are you doing?

Stacey Nothing!
Jimmy Home!
Stacey Dad?
Jimmy I've got drenched coming across here. Come on, let's have you! You
    know I want to go out!

Stacey grabs her bags and walks quickly past her father, and her friends

Stacey I've got to go!
Mary OK!
Jimmy (*to Mary*) Who are you, then?
Mary I, I, I!
Jimmy Spit it out, love, I haven't got all night!
Mary I'm Stacey's dr-drama teacher.
Jimmy Well, she should be at home!

   Jimmy exits

Silence. Mary is shaken

Maggie Show us that dance again, miss, it looked good.
Mary No. I'd better not...
Maggie Oww, I like a laugh!

A beat

Kerry Her dad doesn't like her staying behind.
Maggie You should see her dance, miss, she's brilliant!
Mary Well, I'd better let you go.
Kerry There's no point me going home yet, anyway, my mum'll not be back
    from the hospital till late.
Mary Oh, right.
Kerry That was one of the reasons why I wanted to come here. They want
    you off the grounds as soon as the bell goes. I've got four hours to kill. Can
    I stay here a bit longer?
Mary If you like, but I'll be leaving at half four.
Kerry I know, but I'm freezing! (*She sits and makes herself comfortable*)
Mary So does your mother work at the hospital?
Kerry No, it's my grandma! She's got breast cancer, miss.
Mary Oh.
Kerry And my grandad died last month. So that didn't do her any good.
Mary Oh, I'm sorry about that!

Silence

Kerry Miss, I used to love doing drama.
Mary Did you?
Maggie I didn't.
Kerry Ever since I was little I made stories up.
Mary Everybody does!
Kerry I've got characters and plots and all sorts.
Mary So what's your story, Maggie, what do you do at home?
Maggie Have my tea, and then go to my room.
Mary Don't you go out?
Maggie There's nowhere to go! Is there?
Mary And what do you do, Kerry?
Kerry Eh?
Mary At home?

Music. The Lights change for the song

Song 2: Walking the Dog

Kerry   What do I do at home?
                You want to know?
                What do I do at home?
                You want to know?
  (*Speaking*) Well here goes…

                When I get home from school
                I have a snack
                I have my tea,
                I watch TV
                And at nine o'clock I have another snack
                I snack, that's what I do.
                I sit there on the sofa and I snack.

                Then I sit, just like a blob
                I plug into the box, like I'm a slob.
                I watch the soaps, I watch the vets
                I watch the swapping homes
                And looking after pets.

                I stuff my face like it's a race
                I stuff biscuits in my mouth just to fill the space

                I watch the news,
                It's always war.

Sometimes I wonder what we are educated for.
And there I sit just like a stone
Stuffed full of biscuits and deeply all alone.

Till Mum comes in, and Dad comes back.
Then I run upstairs and have another snack.

I snack, that's what I do
I have me tea and watch TV
And then I snack.
And then sometimes I walk the dog out on the back.

I help my mum
He dun't do owt!
Every night he says this time he's going to slit her throat.
It's just a joke, it's just a phrase.
When he's in that mood it makes me wonder why she stays.
It make me sick,
It makes me crack.
I wish for just this once that she would hit him back.

That's why I snack
That's why I snack
Sometimes I hear the clashing of a smack.
That's when I walk the dog out on the back
That's when I walk the dog out on the back.
That's why I walk the dog out on the back.
That's why I walk the dog out on the back.

Silence. Mary is moved by this song. Kerry and Maggie look at her

   Kerry and Maggie exit

Mary remains on stage. A musical refrain from Walking the Dog. *The Lights fade to Black-out*

SCENE 4

The staff room. Night

Music fades

Mary is on stage but is animated

Tom enters. He has books and papers, even more than we saw before

Tom Well, we get the roof fixed in History and the electricity goes in
Geography. I wouldn't be surprised if the whole school ground to a halt one
day. Ted Brown'll not have much chance of finding darkest Congo down
there today. He'd be lucky if he could find the bloody blackboard rubber!
It's one thing after another, Mrs Clifford! So how are you finding the kids?
Don't tell me, you just open the classroom door and there they are? I jest
of course!

Mary Well, they lack motivation, but…

Tom Motivation, exactly! Car keys? (*He fumbles for his car keys*)

Mary And what they do in their spare time seems … I don't know, empty.

Tom Don't think about it too much, you'll go mad. No matter how much we
try to swing the balance the other way…

A beat

Mary I had three kids turn up for my dance class yesterday!

Tom And there you were desperate for your pot noodle!

Mary Stacey Naylor was one of them. Then her f-father came into school
threatening.

Tom Thick as a brick! I know I shouldn't say that but… In and out of prison.

Mary I mean the girl has obviously got some talent.

Tom At what?

Mary Well, she's a n-natural mover.

Tom Yes, I think half the Year Eleven boys would agree with you there! I
remember Stacey from the Christmas dance. I don't know what she was
wearing, but it was all going on in there!

Mary They're not a bad bunch to be honest. And I th-think they're quite
interested. I don't know if you've seen it, but there are heats for a national
dance competition up in the staff room. I thought if we entered it would be
a little project for them.

Tom is still searching for his keys

Tom Oh no! Where have I put them? Now I had them this morning.

Mary So w-what do you think?

Tom finds his car keys

Tom Ah ah! Well, far be it from me to stop you. I like to encourage anything,
anything to get us off the bottom! I'd even streak if I thought it would help
us. Good grief, what a horrible thought, anyway, good-night!

Mary's mobile rings

> *Three cleaners enter (the three students, although where resources allow, separate dancers could be used) and begin to tidy up as Mary takes the call*

Mary Hallo? Peter? … No, I can talk. … So when did you plan this? Have you asked Jess? … Oh, well, thank you, for consulting with me! … I'm only her mother, for God's sake! I thought that was supposed to be my weekend? … Well, if you think a fifteen year-old girl wouldn't want to go to Paris for the weekend you're softer than I thought. … No, I'm not shouting! … Well, I am her mother! … I'm not shouting, you're the one who's shouting! Oh, stick it, Peter, just stick it! (*She snaps the phone off*)

Cleaner 1 Have you finished in here, love?

Cleaner 2 'Cos we've got to get sorted.

Mary Yes. I'm just about finished!

> *The three cleaners dance a mop dance as Mary exits*

SCENE 5

Marina. Night

We get the impression of a marina quay. A bench is placed on stage. Ripple water effects. Music fades

Jimmy Naylor enters, he is wearing a tracksuit and has been running

Jimmy Oh, hell! (*He sits on somes steps*)

> *Mary enters. She is wrapped up against the cold. She walks down to look at the water*

Don't jump!

Mary Do I look that desperate?

Jimmy Well, the water's freezing.

Mary Oh, right!

Jimmy stands to return to the gym. They notice each other for the first time

It's Mr Naylor? Isn't it?

Jimmy Who wants to know?

Mary You came into my class yesterday.

Jimmy Oh, ay, that's right!

Mary Is Stacey OK?
Jimmy Yes, she's fine!

A beat

Mary Anyway! (*She looks at the water and turns to go*)
Jimmy You a teacher, then?
Mary No, I'm a shepherd.
Jimmy Oh right!
Mary Sorry, yes, I am, yes.
Jimmy Fancy yourself as a bit of a joker, do you?
Mary Sorry!
Jimmy What are you doing down the docks, then?
Mary Just walking. Clearing my head! (*She looks at him and turns to walk away*)
Jimmy She promised me that she'd be home, that's all…
Mary Right!
Jimmy That's why I came for her.
Mary I see.
Jimmy She's only a bit of a kid.
Mary Well, she's…
Jimmy I like to keep my eye on her.
Mary Well, that's…
Jimmy I don't want her getting up to anything, you know what it's like. There's a lot of stuff going down on that estate. Heroin, all bloody sorts!
Mary Really?
Jimmy Next door but one's a dealer, I swear it. There's kids dropping like flies. I don't want Stace around any of that shite!
Mary Absolutely!

A beat

Jimmy Anyway they don't go to school to do that, do they? She can dance all she wants when she's got a job.
Mary That's rr-right! (*She turns to depart*)
Jimmy She any good, then?
Mary Well, she says she's interested.
Jimmy She'll tell you she's interested in going to the moon. If she thought you'd believe her!

A beat

Mary Well, anyway…!

A beat

Jimmy I'd better get back in there before I catch my death. (*He moves to exit*)
Mary So what are you training for, anyway?
Jimmy Me? I'm training for life. That's what I'm training for!

Mary moves to go

Mary Yes, so am I, Mr Naylor. It sounds like we're in the same job. (*She is almost off*)
Jimmy I don't think so, love! I don't bloody think so.

   Jimmy exits

Music plays as the Lights fade to Black-out

SCENE 6

The drama space

Music

The three girls enter. They sit on three chairs, and imagine they are on computers

Stacey Click on.
All Click on.
Stacey Click off!
All Click off!
Stacey Log on!
All Log on!
Stacey Log off!
All Log off!
Stacey On line…
All On line…
Stacey Dot com…
All Dot com…
Stacey Click on…
All Click on…
Stacey Click off.
All Click off.

The dance stops abruptly

Kerry Miss, that's as far as we've got!

Mary Well, it's a start!

Kerry It's supposed to be about the internet, miss.

Mary Yes, well, it's a good starting point, but it needs developing.

Maggie She thinks it's crap!

Mary I don't!

Maggie I think doing drugs is a better idea. Or the end of the world!

Stacey Not.

Maggie Snot.

Mary All right, all right!

Maggie Because it's more realer.

Stacey How is it?

Maggie Because people take drugs.

Stacey Do you?

Maggie No.

Stacey So how is it more realer?

Maggie So what are you, a computer?

The girls start to move to repeat the dance, however a school bell rings, signifying the end of the day

Kerry Oh, can't we just do it again?

Mary No, that's it. I think we'd better leave it there for today.

Stacey I'll have to go anyway! I'll see you!

Mary Stacey, have you got just a minute?

Stacey If I'm late I'm dead!

Mary I need to talk to all of you.

Stacey What about?

Mary Well, there's a couple of things. I don't know how you feel about this, but … I've entered us into a competition.

Stacey A what?

Mary A dance competition.

Maggie What for?

Mary To dance.

Maggie What for, we're crap! We can't enter into a competition, we're shit, look at that, click on, dot com, rubbish! It's rubbish, we made it up in half a minute.

Mary Thank you!

Kerry What competition is it, miss?

Mary Well, there are local heats and if you get through, you go to the final in Birmingham.

Kerry I've never been to Birmingham.

Maggie I have, it's crap!

Stacey And what's the other thing?

Mary Oh right, well, my sister manages a ticket agency, right!

Maggie My sister works for an escort agency, so what?

Mary Well, I was telling her about you three and she thought it would be a good idea if we had a trip to London to watch some modern dance.

Kerry London?

Maggie I've never been to London.

Kerry What sort of modern dance, miss?

Mary Modern, modern dance! She's got these tickets for a matinee at Sadler's Wells and then in the evening she's managed to get four free backstage passes for a show.

Maggie What show?

Mary But if we go, you'll have to show me you're committed to the dance project.

Kerry Is it *The Lion King*?

Mary No, it's not *The Lion King*!

Stacey moves to depart

Kerry Is it *Beauty and the Beast*?

Maggie I've seen that on video. It's shit!

Stacey I've got to go!

Mary OK, I'd better let you go and tell you tomorrow. You've probably never heard of him anyway.

Maggie Is it Cliff Richard?

Kerry He's snot!

Maggie I think he's great.

Kerry Cliff Richard?

Maggie Yes!

Stacey Who is it, then?

Mary Oh, didn't I tell you? It's Robbie Williams!

Stacey stops in her tracks

Stacey What?

Mary I've got four tickets to see Robbie. At Wembley Arena!

A beat

Stacey It's a joke?

Mary Snot!

Maggie Not?

Mary Snot!

Stacey Oh, my…!
Maggie Oh, brilliant!
Stacey Robbie Williams, brilliant!

Stacey runs off stage

Mary So are you interested or what?
Kerry Miss, brilliant.
Mary We've got to get it all sorted yet, but…
Kerry Robbie Williams. I'm taking my autograph book, miss.
Mary Good for you!

A beat

Kerry Miss, how will we get to London?
Mary We'll book the school mini bus!
Kerry Where will we stop?
Maggie Miss, what do you have to wear?
Kerry Miss, will we need spending money?
Maggie Miss, can we smoke?
Kerry Miss, can you take a camera?
Maggie Miss, can we take some cider?
Mary Hang on, hang on, one thing at a time, you've got to ask your parents
    if you can go yet.

They are all beginning to get very excited

Kerry Oh, we're going to see Robbie, I can't believe it.
Maggie I can't…
Kerry Robbie!
Maggie Brilliant!
Kerry Miss, do you like Robbie?
Mary (*mocking a young girl*) Yes, I think he's brilliant. He's my favourite,
    oh, I love him, oh, my God, I can't believe it. I'm going to see Robbie, and
    I've got a backstage pass, I might leave home and go and live with him!
    Argh! Robbie, Robbie, Robbie!

All of them scream and start to jump around chanting as they do so

All Robbie, Robbie, Robbie, Robbie!

Music plays

Black-out

SCENE 7

Stacey's home

Music fades

Jimmy is sitting watching the telly, he has a can of beer in his hand. Stacey stands with her back towards him

As the scene starts she turns to face him

Jimmy No.
Stacey Dad?
Jimmy No.
Stacey Why?
Jimmy Never mind why!

Silence

Stacey Please?
Jimmy (*watching TV*) Have you seen this, it's shite!
Stacey Please?
Jimmy What have I said?
Stacey I know but…?
Jimmy No!
Stacey It's just one night.
Jimmy No.
Stacey I'm sixteen!
Jimmy I know that!
Stacey What do you think I'm going to do?
Jimmy You're not going to do anything because you're not going.
Stacey I am! (*She makes to depart*)

Jimmy looks at her and stirs from the chair

Jimmy Who's going to pay for you, who's going to pay for the hotel or are you going to sleep on the streets?
Stacey Don't be pathetic!
Jimmy You keep on and I'll break every bone in your body in a minute, and you'll be pathetic!
Stacey Go on, then.
Jimmy Robbie Williams? What's so good about him, he's a nobody!
Stacey He's more than you.

Jimmy Oh, shut up, you silly bitch!

Silence

Stacey Please, can I go?
Jimmy No!
Stacey I'm begging you!
Jimmy No…
Stacey Why, why, you haven't told me why?
Jimmy Because, that's why!

Silence. Music plays. Jimmy sits. Stacey moves into a separate area but they sing to each other

Song 3: Where Did Love Go?

Jimmy   She seems so young but how she's grown
                   Though her eyes are on the world to me she's still a child.
                   I need her here I couldn't be alone.
                   But I know one day she'll leave. Can we ever be reconciled?
                   I thought this love would last forever
                   I thought our dreams would pull us through.
                   I thought the ties that bind would keep us close together
                   I thought I'd always love you!

Stacey   Where did love go?
                   I'd like to know
                   Why did love die?
                   Please, please, tell me why!

                   I thought this love would last a lifetime!

Jimmy   And I thought that love would see us through.
                   What can I say to you?

Stacey   There is nothing you could say
                   And there is nothing you could do
                   'Cos every time you reel me in, you push me away
                   When I'm the one
                   The only one who ever really cared about you.

Jimmy   Where did love go?
Stacey   All I need is some time to myself

Jimmy   Can't you tell me, I'd like to know.
Stacey   Then maybe we could give it a try.
Jimmy   And why does love die?
Stacey   But with you it's always now or never
Jimmy & Stacey Please won't you tell me why!

Key change in music, guitar solos over the following

> Why does love die?
> Please, please, tell us why
> Does love just fade?
> Why does it fade away to a colder and darker shade?

Stacey   I thought our love would last a lifetime.
Jimmy   And I thought our love would pull us through.
Jimmy & Stacey I thought that blood was thicker than forever.
> But will I always love you?

Jimmy and Stacey look at each other. The Lights fade on them as they exit

SCENE 8

Staff room

Music fades

Tom enters with Mary, he has even more files and papers than we have seen him with before

Tom Are you sure you want to be in London for a weekend with Year Eleven cast-offs? I mean, I've just come across the Three Musketeers on Biology cover. Stacey Naylor and Maggie Brooke together, oh dear me! Burke and Hare weren't as frightening!

Mary But you're not against it in pr-principle, are you?

Tom I'm not against it, but I'm sure there are more deserving cases. I mean, you want to take three absolute "woodentops" just because they turned up for your dance group! They haven't got a blessed clue, that group! School means nothing to them. And science? They think science is all about sex education! The birds and the bloody bees! It's all they want to know about! You just can't make science make sense to them! I mean where would we be without science?

Mary Where would we be without art?

Tom Sorry?

Mary I said where would we be without art?

Tom Well, yes, but we're not training artists, though, are we?

Mary No, but...?

Tom We're lucky if we can potty train some of them, I jest etc., but...!

Mary We ought to be training people to participate.

Tom What?

Mary Don't you think we should be developing people so they can be better human beings?

Tom With any luck! But it's heavy going out there today!

Mary And artistic expression's crucial!

Tom But you can't measure what the kids are getting out of it!

Mary Well, it's not always black and white.

Tom Exactly!

Mary So are you saying the arts are not worth having?

Tom Well, I can live without a school full of kite making and potato printing, thanks very much!

Mary When I was last in school, drama was absolutely central to school life!

Tom Do you know why they changed from all that airy fairy stuff to the National Curriculum? They were following the Japanese model. We needed a strong science base to compete. We still do!

Mary But we don't want a nation without artists?

Tom Artists come out of the woodwork, from, under stones, that's what they do, by their very nature!

Mary A lot of those Japanese k-kids who went to university, are experiencing breakdowns because they didn't have an expressive education.

Tom Well, that's as maybe!

Mary All I'm saying is, we should have a balanced curriculum.

Tom What, just like that, hey presto, etc.?

Mary Then maybe we'd turn out well-balanced individuals.

Tom Oh, tosh!

Mary Sorry?

Tom Tosh!

Mary Well, what about if we actually had a society with good schools, good health services and good theatres so all these well-educated, and healthy people have somewhere to go to at night! Instead of being stuck in the bloody house, stuffing their faces in front of the box!

Tom Well, I don't know where you taught before, Mrs Clifford, but this is the real world! That's what people do! You're living in a bubble, love!

Mary Well, I've seen what the arts can do!

Tom All you ever get from the arts is "save us, save us"! It's the same old story, love. If they're not cost effective, close them down.

Mary Like failing schools?

Tom The arts didn't help anyone in Belsen, love!

Mary They didn't kill anyone either!

Tom The point I'm trying to make is; you could close all the theatres tomorrow and no-one would bat an eyelid! But if you closed all the hospitals, and the twenty-four hour chemists there would be an uproar, etc.!

Mary Well, look, I don't use the chemists, I'm homeopathic, so you can close them all for me! And I'm in a private scheme, so you can shut all the NHS hospitals, as far as I'm concerned!

Tom Absolute tosh!

Mary Exactly! Just because you don't go, doesn't mean we shouldn't have them?

Tom But why should we support them?

Mary We want a better society, don't we? Isn't that why you're here?

Tom Look, it's simple; the arts aren't as important! Full stop, ask anybody! They're a nice little pastime!

Mary Oh, shut up, you silly man!

Tom Well, actually, Mrs Clifford, I would prefer it if you referred to me as Headmaster and not the familiar!

Mary I'm sorry.

A beat

Tom Well, anyway!

Mary Maybe it was too big a topic for first break?

Tom Yes, well, nice to speak with you. But anyway, mustn't stand around all day, up and at them, etc.!

A beat

Mary So do you think it would be possible to book the school mini bus?

Tom The mini bus, the mini bus. A scientific invention of course! I jest. When for?

Mary A week on Saturday?

Tom Let me consult my mini bus book. You could be lucky! (*He looks in his mini bus book*) Agh!

Mary Is there a problem?

Tom It's booked. Foxy's got a basketball training session in Huddersfield.

Mary Oh, right!

Tom Sorry.

Mary Is there just the one?

Tom It took us three sponsored walks to get that. (*He looks back at his book*) No, that doesn't look like it's going to work out. Pity about that! Sorry. I need to see Foxy actually, I'll need to get some tickets if they reach the final. Shame about the mini bus.

Tom exits

Silence. Mary sits alone

Jimmy Naylor enters

Jimmy Have you got a minute?
Mary Well … yes…

A beat

Jimmy Well, me and Stacey were on about this London thing, right!
Mary Oh, good!
Jimmy But she says she doesn't want to go.
Mary Oh, right!
Jimmy She's a bit shy about telling you, after you've got the tickets and all that. So I said I'd come and…
Mary I see.
Jimmy She's all over the shop at the moment. Doesn't know what she wants.
Mary Oh dear!
Jimmy I mean she's only been back in school a month, hasn't she? Best if she gets settled in.
Mary Yes, it would probably be better for her.
Jimmy She says she can't be bothered going all the way down to London.
Mary Right!
Jimmy So anyway! Sorry about that … but she just asked would I…
Mary No, no, right!
Jimmy Now you know!
Mary Well, thanks for coming to tell me! I suppose it's hardly surprising really.
Jimmy What is?
Mary Her not wanting to go to London with a teacher she doesn't know.
Jimmy Yes, well, you know what kids are like. They think it's a good idea at the time.
Mary I should have known better. But since it would be a once in a lifetime ch-chance I thought I'd try it.
Jimmy You've got to try things.
Mary Because you never know, we might discover that the world's not flat. But then again we mi-might get to Doncaster and fall off, end up in New Zealand or somewhere!

Jimmy I'm not thick, love.

Mary Nobody said anything about anybody being thick.

Jimmy I don't think I like your attitude.

Mary Well, I'm sorry, but...

Jimmy Listen, love...

Mary Sa-save your br-breath, Mr Naylor, because it looks like the trip is going to be off, anyway. The Head would prefer it if I gave the tickets to some students who are more deserving!

Jimmy Right.

Mary Well, anyway, thanks for coming in!

A beat

Jimmy I don't feel too bad about her not going now!

Mary Anyway.

Jimmy Yes, right!

Mary I'd better get on. I'm sure you're extremely busy! (*She makes to exit*)

Jimmy You know, now I know why I always hated school.

Mary Me too, Mr Naylor, me too!

Mary walks off

Jimmy watches her go. Music plays. The Lights fade

Scene 9

Drama studio

Music fades

Maggie looks out of the drama studio for Mary. Kerry hangs about aimlessly. Stacey is sat separate

Maggie Where is she, then? This lesson is nearly finished, isn't it?

Kerry Why won't he let you go, anyway?

Stacey Because!

Maggie Anyway, just because she's not coming doesn't mean we can't go! I'll ask our Stephanie if she wants your ticket.

Stacey Oh, right!

The girls start to get loud, Maggie and Stacey creating a tense atmosphere

Maggie Why, do you expect us not to go!

Stacey No!
Maggie Yes!
Stacey Snot!
Maggie (*forcefully*) Bog!
Stacey I might go, anyway.
Maggie Bog!

Mary enters, already stressed

Mary What's all the noise? I can hear shouting half-way down the corridor.
  What's going on? I thought I told you to get on with your project, if I was
  ever late?
Maggie Miss, we have.
Mary It doesn't sound like it!
Kerry Miss, are we still going to London?
Mary Let's just leave that!
Kerry Miss, are we though?
Mary Kerry?
Kerry Miss, are we though?

Mary explodes

Mary Just shut up for one minute, will you?

A beat

Kerry Are we though, miss?
Maggie Stacey can't go, miss!
Kerry Are we though, miss?
Mary If I can get the mini bus, yes!
Maggie What do you mean if?
Mary If I can get the mini bus back off Mr F-Fox the Ba-Basketball man,
  yes!
Maggie Our Steph'll have Stacey's ticket!
Mary Let's just leave that for one minute!
Stacey Do you want a smack in the gob?
Maggie What, off you?
Stacey Yes!
Maggie Bog!
Stacey Not!
Maggie Double bog!
Mary (*shouting*) Can we just hang on!

Silence

Maggie Bog!
Stacey Not!
Mary (*strongly*) Pack it in! Act your age.
Kerry Not your shoe size!
Mary Kerry?
Kerry (*sheepishly*) It's a song.
Mary I know it's a song!
Kerry (*sheepishly*) Tom Jones.

A beat

Mary So you haven't done anything?
Stacey No, miss!
Mary You've been sat here doing nothing for a whole lesson?
Maggie What's the point doing our project if Stacey can't do it?
Mary Well, what about the fact that it's going to be part of your coursework?
Kerry Miss, are we still going to London?
Mary Shut up, Kerry Shields. Just shut up, will you, please!
Kerry Are we going though, miss?
Mary What about the f-f-fact, that you are going to be assessed on it? What about the f-f-fact that you should be actually doing something, rather than f-f-farting about all lesson doing sod all?
Kerry Miss, you said farting.
Mary I bend over backwards and you just won't help yourselves. You've got no discipline, no loyalty, you're not interested in anything, are you?
Stacey No!
Mary I thought we were doing well! Well, if you won't help me, then I won't help you. I can't see any point in us going to London. I'll give the tickets to some of the other Year Eleven kids who actually do something in school, shall I?
Stacey Might as well!
Mary I thought you were supposed to be interested? I'm fighting for you in the staff room and you've let me down.
Maggie Miss, you've let us down, by not booking the bloody mini bus in front of F-Foxy.
Mary Well, if you had some respect for yourselves you might just find that others would have r-r-respect for you! I mean what have you done this lesson, absolutely sod all! And you're not bothered, are you?

Silence. The bell rings

Kerry Miss, the bell's gone.
Mary How observant, th-thank you, Kerry Shields, winner of this year's

Common Road High School "stating the bl-bloody obvious" co-competition!

Maggie Miss, we've got Mr Harding and he goes mad if we're late.

Mary Well, you'd better go, then, hadn't you?

Kerry So that's it, then, we're not going?

Mary No.

Silence

Maggie Well, thanks a lot, Mrs Stammerer!

A beat

Kerry Miss, grown-ups are shit sometimes!

A beat

Mary Yes, they are!

The trio of girls drift out of the drama studio

Silence

Jimmy enters slowly

Jimmy So this is what you do? Sit about all day, what a job! (*He looks around the studio*) Need some new chairs, don't you? This stuff's ruined!

Mary Well, there you go.

Jimmy Oh ay, I went to a school like this.

Mary And you hated it!

Jimmy What sort of school did you go to?

Mary I went to a sc-school like this. Worse than this actually!

Jimmy Come off it.

Mary P-Please yourself!

A beat

Jimmy So Stacey doesn't deserve to go to London, then? That's what they're saying, is that right?

Mary That's right!

Jimmy What if I said she could go!

Mary I thought you said she didn't w-want to?

Jimmy Ay, I did.

Mary I thought you said she'd made her own mind up?
Jimmy Don't be smart with me, love!

A beat

Mary Well, I'm afraid she's had it, because we can't get a mini bus, and I haven't had time to book anywhere to stay!

Silence

Jimmy What if I got a mini bus?
Mary Sorry?
Jimmy What if I got you a mini bus?
Mary Well...
Jimmy What if I drove you down there?

A beat

Mary No, that's kind of you, Mr Naylor, but we can't...
Jimmy I only offer the once!

A beat

Mary No, we'd better leave it.
Jimmy Fair enough!
Mary I mean, I've still got to find somewhere to stay and...
Jimmy How many?
Mary Sorry?
Jimmy How many of you are going?
Mary Well, there's the three girls and me, and whoever drives, but...!
Jimmy Do you want to leave it with me?
Mary Well, I...?
Jimmy I could get something sorted!
Mary But how much would it cost? Where would we stay? I think we'd better forget it!
Jimmy Leave it with me, I know people!

Jimmy exits

Mary is left alone. Silence

Mary Yes, but what kind of people?

Song 4: Break Away

The girls enter with rucksacks and suitcases

Jimmy enters with a holdall and a steering wheel

Stacey	We're stepping out of the darkness
Kerry	Driving out of the grey.
Maggie	Having a change from boring things
All Girls	'Cos we're going to break away!
	We're stepping out of the nowhere
	We'll leave the weeds in the yard
	Breaking away from the daily grind.
Kerry	Let me tell you it's not hard.
All Girls	'Cos we're gunna break away
	Yes we're gunna break
Stacey	Gunna break
All Girls	Gunna break away,
	If only for a day!
Stacey	Let's let the damp walls stay here
	Let the wallpaper peel
Kerry & Maggie	Gunna go to the big bright lights
Stacey	Just to see if it's real!
All Girls	We feel the pull of the city
	We'll touch the heart of the smoke
	We've never felt so alive.
Kerry	And let me tell you it's no joke.
Maggie	We're stepping out of the smallness
Stacey	Stepping into the light
Kerry	Leave my parents at home to slog it all out!
Stacey	Let them fight into the night.

Kerry & Stacey	Can you feel the freedom?
Maggie	Feel the wind as we drive?
All Girls	Going to make it a big fun time,
	From the moment we arrive!

'Cos we're going to break away
Yes we're gunna break
Gunna break
Gunna break away.
If only for a day!

Kerry & Stacey Never felt such excitement

All Girls   Never felt so free
                   Never felt so good in my life!
Mary & Girls Is this happening to me?
All   We're stepping out of the darkness.
                   Driving out from the grey,
                   Can't believe that we're going
                   We've packed our bags we're on our way.

                   'Cos we're gunna break away
                   We're gunna break away
                   We're gunna break away
                   We're gunna break away
                   We're gunna break away
                   We're gunna break away
                   If only for a day.
                   Break away!

Black-out

CURTAIN

ACT II

PROLOGUE

The Concert. Night

The prologue opens in darkness. Music fades up, and gets louder and louder

A spotlight picks out the three girls. Mary has a separate spotlight. They are all at the Robbie Williams concert. We see a sequence of flashing lights. The girls are screaming and going mad within the confines of their spotlights. Mary is also enjoying the concert. Mary is behaving as if she was a sixteen year old. They move in slow motion, all facial expressions are exaggerated. The whole cast begin to chant. They start slowly and then build to a climax

All Robbie, Robbie, Robbie, Robbie! (*Repeat 11 times*)

On the final chant they freeze in a big triumphant gesture. Music plays. Slowly the images crumble, and tiredness sets in. The Lights fade to Black-out

SCENE 1

The Astoria Hotel. Night

Music fades and the Lights come up on the lounge area of a very seedy London hotel, the Astoria

The three girls and Mary are standing exactly where they were, but we now see that they have their baggage with them. The girls are tired. Mary is drunk but trying to keep it together. She is wearing a scarf. The Irish landlord, Ronnie, a very seedy man with glasses with an eye blacked out, stands and views his new clients

Jimmy enters, carrying a number of bags

Ronnie addresses the lot of them

Ronnie What the bloody hell time do you call this? I've been waiting for you since seven o'clock. I've let your rooms go twice! What do you think I'm running here?

Jimmy Sorry, Ronnie mate!

Ronnie A right bloody carry on and no mistake! So what have we got here, then, your own little fan club, is it?

Jimmy I wouldn't go that far!

Ronnie So where have you been till now, tell me that!

Jimmy The Robbie Williams concert!

Ronnie Bloody hell, man! Will you watch any old shite?

Jimmy I didn't see it, but…

Ronnie I like the Dubliners and everything else can just take a running jump! Have you seen the Dubliners' girls? Oh ay, now there's a band for you… Or Flanagan and Allen! Have you ever seen them?

Jimmy Can we get these kids checked in, Ronnie?

Ronnie You've got some lovely looking girls here as well, that you have!

Mary Ask him if the bar's still open?

Ronnie Lovely little things all of them.

Jimmy Can we get them checked in?

Mary Ask him if there's a late bar?

Jimmy You've had enough!

Mary staggers about the hotel

Mary I'll just have another brandy. (*She slips into a chair*)

Kerry Are you drunk, miss?

Mary Me?

Ronnie and Jimmy are together

Ronnie So who've we got here, then?

Jimmy Don't worry, she's not one of the kids! They've not touched a drop.

Ronnie Well, I only have one good eye but I can see that.

Jimmy She's the teacher.

Ronnie The teacher?

Jimmy Oh ay, what an example, eh?

Ronnie Bloody hell, I thought she was a hooker!

Jimmy Get off!

Ronnie No, honest to God! I thought you'd brought your own.

Jimmy Let's get these kids sorted, Ronnie, can we?

Mary calls over to Ronnie

Mary Have you got a brandy, love?

Ronnie A bloody teacher, is she? Honest to God, and I thought we could make some money out of her. A double did you say, lady?

Jimmy Ronnie?

Ronnie Are you not having one, Jimmy?

Jimmy Let's get these sorted, they're dead on their bloody feet.

Mary shouts to Jimmy

Mary Oh, let them stay up a bit!

Jimmy It's a quarter to two, he's wanting to get locked up, aren't you?

Ronnie Oh, don't mind me, for goodness' sake! Let the girls have a tot, it'll not kill 'em, now will it? It's medicinal, for goodness' sake. My sister's kids were on whiskey since they were five. Alcoholics now, all three of 'em, but there you go!

Jimmy Ronnie?

Ronnie I'll get the lady a brandy, and four whiskeys, I'll have one myself with the girls.

Jimmy No, you won't, they're going to bed.

Ronnie exits

Jimmy moves to address the trio

Maggie Can't we just have a brandy and a smoke, Mr Naylor?

Jimmy Can you bloody hell!

Stacey Oh, that man says we can have a drink.

Jimmy Never mind what he says. He'll say bloody anything. You've been out all day, let's get you checked in!

Mary I'm just going to have a nightcap!

Maggie I always have a whiskey before I go to bed.

Jimmy Well, you're not having one with me about.

Stacey How old do you think we are?

Jimmy Never mind how old you are.

Mary Let them have five minutes!

Jimmy They look bloody washed out the lot of them! Get your bags and let's get you sorted.

The girls pick up their luggage

Maggie When I phoned my mum I got these cards from the telephone booth, what are they for, then? (*She offers Jimmy a number of call girl cards*)

Jimmy Never mind them, I'll take them. I don't want you going back home with anything like that! Come on, let's have you. All decent people were in bed hours ago.

Mary shouts from her chair

Mary Did he say he was getting me a brandy?
Kerry Is Mrs Clifford drunk?
Jimmy No, she's just tired.
Kerry She looks drunk to me.
Jimmy And how would you know?
Kerry My mum's like that every night.
Jimmy Is she, now!
Kerry Worse than that.

The girls are hovering with no intention of going to bed

Mary What did you think of Robbie?
Kerry Brilliant!
Maggie I thought the dance was better!
Stacey Yes, that was brilliant!

Ronnie enters with a large brandy and one for himself

Ronnie A large brandy for the teacher! Don't mind if I join you, do you? Now here's a woman after my own heart. Are you married, darling?
Jimmy Ronnie?
Ronnie Right, coming straight away! Let's get these little chickens tucked up in bed, shall we? Would any of you girls like a little hand with your luggage there? Can I help anybody at all?
Jimmy Ronnie?
Ronnie I'm only asking, I'm only asking.
Jimmy Ay, I know.
Ronnie Does anybody want a little tonic bringing up before they get their little heads down?
Jimmy Ronnie, they're sixteen.
Ronnie Are they? Well, isn't that wonderful! Up you go now, girls, I'll come and open the doors momentarily. Rooms twelve and thirteen. Unlucky for some! I've put you close together. In case you get scared during the night, or you have bad dreams and you have to get in bed with each other!
Jimmy Ronnie?
Ronnie Will you and the lady be in the one room, Jim? I can save on washing if that's the case?
Jimmy I don't think so!

Ronnie attempts to shepherd the girls off

Ronnie I'll be in room eleven, so if any of you need me during the night, for goodness' sakes just give me a knock, all right?

Maggie What's he like?
Kerry He's like my uncle!
Jimmy Right, how many times. Good grief, who'd be a teacher? You've done what you've wanted all day, now come on!
Stacey Oh Dad, you're boring!
Jimmy Tough.
Stacey Why can't we stay up with Mrs Clifford?
Kerry Sometimes I stay up all night.
Jimmy Well, you're not doing that here.
Stacey Why can't we?
Jimmy Because it's a big bad world, that's why.

Music begins to play under

Stacey What?
Jimmy It's a big bad world.
Stacey A big bad world?
Jimmy Yes!

Stacey picks up the phrase and turns it so that it becomes sexy and vampish. The other girls join in what is a provocative dance routine and strongly aggressive song

Stacey   It's a big bad, big bad, big bad world!
               It's a big bad, big bad world!

Song 5: Big Bad World

All join in, speaking over the music

All   Yes, it's a big bad, big bad, big bad world,
               It's a big bad, big bad world!

Stacey   It's a big bad world,
               But we want to stay up
               It's a big bad, big bad world!

Maggie   We're not little women,
               We're not little girls!
               It's a big bad big bad world!

Kerry   We're not wearing nappies,
               Or our hair in curls!
               It's a big bad, big bad world!

Stacey	Don't put us to bed
Maggie	Don't send us to sleep.
All	It's a big bad, big bad world!

(Singing) It's a big bad, big bad, big bad world
It's a big bad, big bad world!

It's a big bad, big bad big bad world
It's a big bad, big bad world!

Stacey *(speaking)* We're not scared of the
All *(speaking)* city
Stacey *(speaking)* Or blinded by
All *(speaking)* lights!
          (Singing) It's a big bad, big bad world!

Maggie *(speaking)* We don't want to
All *(speaking)* sleep,
Maggie *(speaking)* We want to see some more
All *(speaking)* sights!
          (Singing) It's a big bad, big bad world!

Kerry	We want adventures,
Stacey	We want to have dreams
Maggie	We want to have lovers
All	You know what that means!

  (Speaking) Don't think that we're thick
Maggie *(speaking)* Don't keep us at
All *(speaking)* school
          (Singing) It's a big bad, big bad world!

It's a big bad, big bad, big bad world.
It's a big bad, big bad world!

It's a big bad, big bad, big bad world.
It's a big bad, big bad world!

Kerry *(overlapping Maggie and Stacey)* It's a big bad world
                    but we want to grow up
                    It's a big bad big bad
                    big bad big bad world!
Maggie   We know what we're doing
                    When we act the fool.

Maggie & Stacey It's a big bad, big bad world.

Instrumental/dance break

Stacey	It's a big
All	bad,
Stacey	big
All	bad,
Stacey	big bad world,
	It's a big bad, big bad world.
	It's a big juicy, rotten, awful world!
	But now we want to grow up!

The girls are exhausted now, and back where they started on stage before the song

Jimmy No, bugger off. Bed now! The lot of you!

There is a choric groan from the trio. Ronnie commences shepherding them off stage

Ronnie Right, let's have you! I mean upstairs. Let's have you upstairs! Now everyone watch the stairs, and you had all better go to the top before me, in case any of you fall, for goodness' sake. Now we wouldn't want that, would we?

Ronnie and the girls exit

Silence. Mary sips her brandy. Jimmy lights a cigarette

Mary He seems like a nice bloke.
Jimmy Ronnie?
Mary A good bloke!
Jimmy He's a pervert, I don't know about a good bloke!

A beat

Mary What's wrong?
Jimmy What's wrong? My nerves are all over the bloody shop, that's what's wrong!
Mary Why's that, then?
Jimmy With you, woman, you're a bloody headcase. I'm stuck with three kids who're half dressed and a teacher who's half pissed, I mean, come on!

Mary What?
Jimmy You're a mess.
Mary You should see me when I'm really drunk.
Jimmy I don't think you've set much of an example!
Mary Oh, they love it!

A beat

Jimmy Look at you!
Mary What?
Jimmy Drunken women, there's nothing worse!
Mary Oh, shut up!
Jimmy Lovely!

A beat

Mary Anyway, I'm celebrating!
Jimmy Are you?
Mary (*stoically*) Because I'm getting divorced! What about that?
Jimmy It doesn't surprise me!
Mary Anyway, you've some need to talk, look where we're staying?
Jimmy What did you expect for ten quid a night?
Mary (*sipping brandy*) Oh, this is a bit rough! Oh, well! (*She knocks back her brandy*) Oh hell, takes the bloody skin off!
Jimmy Look at you!
Mary What about me?
Jimmy You are not fit to be a teacher!
Mary I'm not, I can tell you, it's knackering!
Jimmy Oh, forget it!
Mary Oh, shut up!
Jimmy Pathetic!
Mary You're only jealous because you're not drunk.
Jimmy You're not fit to teach my kid.

A beat

Mary I'll tell you something, I had the best exam results in the bloody region, when I was teaching, so don't you tell me that I'm not fit to teach! Mind you, they made a fatal mistake. They put me on exam invigilation for my own subject!
Jimmy A cheat and a drunk, then?
Mary Well, at least I'm not boring!
Jimmy My teachers were. Bored me to tears!

Mary Oh, shut up!
Jimmy You're pathetic, love.
Mary Am I?
Jimmy Pathetic!
Mary I bet you've done some crazy things, eh, Jimmy?
Jimmy What?
Mary I bet you've lived a bit! What's the craziest thing you've done, then?
Jimmy Bring a group of kids to London with a teacher who's a sad drunk!

Mary belches

What have we bloody got here?
Mary (*with a Scottish accent*) Oh, you're no too bad, Jimmy, you fancy
  yourself a bit, but you're no too bad. Hey, give us a ciggy, Jimmy, hey
  Jimmy, just a wee ciggy!
Jimmy You're drunk!
Mary And you're an ex-con!
Jimmy That's right.
Mary And in the morning I'll be sober.
Jimmy Winston Churchill!
Mary Very good!
Jimmy I'm no stupid!
Mary Where did you get the van from?
Jimmy Borrowed it.
Mary Oh, boring! It would have been more exciting if you'd have nicked it.
Jimmy No. I didn't!
Mary Well, that's a bit of a let down! I thought you lot were supposed to be
  wild and adventurous?

A beat

Jimmy Well, I'm banned from driving if that's any good!
Mary Well, it's a start.
Jimmy Anyway, don't worry about it.
Mary I'm not, except if anybody finds out…?
Jimmy Nobody will find out, otherwise they'll find out you were drunk in
  loco parentis!
Mary Oh, in loco parentis? That is a big word.
Jimmy Three words!

A beat

Mary Banned from driving? I thought we were going slow, never got in the
  bloody fast lane, did we?

Jimmy Piss off!

A beat

Mary Oh, loosen up a bit! You've got to play a bit, Jim lad! Oh arr, Jim lad!
Jimmy What are you on? (*He makes to exit*)
Mary Do you know why dogs play?
Jimmy What are you on?
Mary Do you know why a dog plays with a bone? He's practising.
Jimmy What for?
Mary Life!
Jimmy Is that right?
Mary He gets a bone, buries it, rolls around with it, fights with it, buries it
and then the next day he goes to find where he's put it and goes through
the whole thing again. He's practising!
Jimmy Know a lot about dogs, do you?
Mary We play as kids but then we stop doing it. We close up! We should
keep playing, all through our lives. It's crucial. It's the only practice for life
we ever get. We've got to play more, Jimmy.

A beat

Jimmy I've always tried to live in the real world.
Mary Well, that's your problem.
Jimmy Ay, that's right.

Mary is now getting loud and presenting herself to Jimmy

Mary No room for romance!
Jimmy That's about it.
Mary No room for the fantastical to happen!
Jimmy Shut up, you silly arse!
Mary You shut up.
Jimmy You shut up, woman.
Mary You shut up and give us a kiss, man!
Jimmy What?
Mary Come on here, give us a bloody kiss, we're on holiday, for goodness'
sake! (*She grabs Jimmy and kisses him*)

He is shocked

There, what about that, I feel so bloody free tonight, I feel so bloody
excited, two brilliant shows, weren't they?

Jimmy I think you should go to bed.
Mary I'll go to bed when I'm ready!

Jimmy turns

Jimmy Well, I'm going to bed!
Mary (*loudly*) Did you like Pina Bausch?
Jimmy Eh?
Mary The dance piece?
Jimmy Ay, not bad.
Mary Sexy, eh?
Jimmy Ay, it was all right.
Mary (*partly to herself*) Good dance is always sexy, really! It's one of the
   main ingredients!
Jimmy I thought the blokes looked a bit wet, but…

A beat

Mary I think Stacey's got a talent, you know?
Jimmy So she's a good dancer, so what, so was I.

A beat

Mary Can I ask you something?
Jimmy If it's what is the capital of New Zealand, you've got me.
Mary I just wanted to test you on something.
Jimmy To make me feel thick?
Mary I don't make you feel thick, do I?
Jimmy You don't make me feel anything, to be honest!
Mary I asked the kids this the other day.

A beat

   What's it like to be blind?
Jimmy Eh?
Mary What's it like to be blind?
Jimmy What sort of daft question is that? Well, it's obvious, isn't it?
Mary Is it?
Jimmy Well, you can't see, can you?
Mary Are you sure?
Jimmy What, is it a trick question or something?

Mary stands and offers her scarf to Jimmy

Mary Here, put this on!
Jimmy What?
Mary Put this on.
Jimmy Piss off yourself!
Mary Put it on over your eyes.
Jimmy What are you gunna do?
Mary Just put it on. I do this in my lessons sometimes.

Jimmy reluctantly puts on the scarf. Mary ties it behind his head

Jimmy Why are you trying to justify yourself to me? I'm a nobody! Now, look at this, now I definitely know it's a waste of time!

Jimmy is now blindfolded. Mary walks away from him

   Ronnie enters

Ronnie All in their bedrooms, bless 'em. I showed them where the shower was but ... what the bloody hell's going on here?

A beat

Mary It's just a game!
Ronnie Ay, that's what they all say, love. I get us all another drink. It looks like we all need one!

   Ronnie exits

Mary Right, come to me!
Jimmy Eh?
Mary Follow my voice and come to me.
Jimmy Where are you?
Mary Find me.
Jimmy This is bloody ridiculous. (*He tries to get over to where Mary is standing, he finds it difficult and suddenly the fun has gone out of the experiment. He is struggling to listen and moves at a snail's pace*) Well, talk then!
Mary Come and find me!
Jimmy Well, this is just... (*He walks into the furniture. He is lost and frustrated*)
Mary Keep coming.
Jimmy Well, this is a right load of bollocks, this is! (*He takes the blindfold off. He is annoyed*) What's the point?

Mary So what's it like?

Jimmy Oh, shut up, woman, making a bloody fool of me!

Mary What's it like being blind, then?

Jimmy I don't know, it must be bloody awful! You don't know where you are, you've got to rely on other people. You feel absolutely isolated. You lose all confidence! I almost broke my neck on the bloody chair, did you see that?

Mary Well, that's a better answer.

Jimmy Yes, but…

Mary Yes, but what…

Jimmy I wasn't thinking before.

Mary Oh, right.

A beat

Jimmy Oh, you think you're smart, don't you? Yes, very good, I'll give you that! That's what you do, then, is it? Make people think? A bit bloody dangerous, I would have thought!

Mary Just imagine what it would be like if we co-could get kids to actually understand, even in a small way how other people f-felt. If we just didn't always give the p-pat answer.

Jimmy It'll not get you a job though! "How many A levels have you got?" "None but I know how a blind man feels!" Oh ay, very well qualified, go to the top of the class.

Mary What's the point having qualifications if you don't know what it feels like to be human?

Jimmy Did you hear me? I was well away, wasn't I?

A beat

I used to tell the tale you know, when I was a young kid. I was always telling the tale, making stories up, because that's what lies are, you know? All the tales I told me dad, oh hell, terrible liar, terrible.

Mary Well anyway…

A beat

Jimmy No more lessons for today?

Mary No, I think you've had enough for one day, I don't want to overload you.

Jimmy Ay, it's shame we've got to go back.

Mary Back to reality?

Jimmy That's right!

A beat

Mary Well, I'd better say good-night then!
Jimmy Ay, well.
Mary Good-night!

A beat

Jimmy Ay, well, good-night!

Music. Jimmy and Mary finish their drinks and begin to tidy away the setting

   Stacey, Kerry and Maggie enter

The girls watch and begin to sing. Slowly they move DS

Song 6: Birds and Bees

Girls	Unless we're mistaken
	Something's going on
	Something is happening.
Stacey	Unless we're mistaken
Maggie	Unless we're wrong
Kerry	There seems to be more to this.
Stacey	Unless we're
Maggie & Kerry Mistaken	
Stacey	It must have been that drunken kiss

All	Unless we're misguided
	They shouldn't get on at all
	No chance, no way!
Stacey	She should have left
Maggie	She should have left and walked away
Stacey	But unless we're
Maggie & Kerry Mistaken,	
Stacey	They really don't know what to say!

Maggie & Kerry Unless we're mistaken.
Stacey They'll stand around like that all day.
Maggie & Kerry Unless we're mistaken
Stacey Like that, without a word to say.

Maggie But it could be a kind of illusion

Stacey	A trick performed with light
Maggie & Kerry	Performed with light
Stacey	And smoke
	Yes it might be a kind of illusion
All	Is this an unkind joke?

Stacey	They seem so odd together
Maggie & Kerry	So odd
	Each not knowing how to please
Stacey	And they seem all misshapen
Maggie & Kerry	Seem all
	The perfect mix of chalk and cheese.

Stacey	Unless we're
Maggie & Kerry	Mistaken
Stacey	There'll always be more days like these
	But I'm sure we're mistaken
Maggie & Kerry	Mistaken
Stacey	'Cos we don't know 'bout the birds and bees
Maggie & Kerry	No, we don't know about the birds and bees.
Stacey	We don't know about the birds and trees
Maggie & Kerry	No, we don't know about the birds and
All	Seas.
Stacey	We could be mistaken
All	But when it comes to the birds and bees
	We don't know
	We were all away that day!

Music ends

The girls exit

The Lights change. Jimmy and Mary are still together. Mary hiccups. Musical sting

Jimmy and Mary exit

The Lights fade to Black-out

SCENE 2

The headmaster's office. Day

A strong spotlight picks out Tom in his office, frustrated. Mary stands close by

Tom I just do not believe it! I am completely speechless! What if something had happened, and it came out that we'd let three children go to London with a man who had only come out of prison four months ago?

Mary He happens to be a good bloke!

Tom I'm told by Mavis that he hasn't even got a driving licence.

Mary Well...

Tom Her husband is the magistrate who banned him!

Mary He's not a bad driver actually!

Tom Apparently there's all kinds of stories about them running riot, getting drunk, and stopping up till all hours! Little Kerry Shields was caught shoplifting from Harrods by all accounts!

Mary Yes, I can explain that! That whole Harrods thing was a mistake!

Tom The whole trip was a mistake. I was against it right from the start, and you know I was!

Mary You didn't actually come out and say, though...!

Tom And where did you stay?

Mary We ... got a deal on a place!

Tom And where did the mini bus come from?

Mary Oh, yes, that, well...

Tom I shudder to think!

Mary That was all above board!

A beat

Tom (*exasperatedly*) I don't know!

Mary You know some of those kids had never been to Leeds before, let alone London.

Tom I know that. I'm not saying that part of it is wrong!

Mary Some of them have never b-been to Doncaster. Kerry Shields had only b-been off their estate eight times in her life!

Tom I know all that, but I mean, Mary, honestly!

A beat

Mary I'm not saying it was all organized, and planned down to the last detail...

Tom ...Because it obviously wasn't.

Mary …but you've got to say "no harm done".
Tom Have I?
Mary No harm done!

A beat

Tom Don't ever, ever pull a trick like this again! My neck is on the line here, you're only here part-time, for goodness' sake! We've got to be accountable, we're responsible for these young people and I don't like the hare-brained idea of shipping them off to London with a convict. I mean who do you think you are, Charles Dickens? Don't ever pull a stunt like that again! Now consider yourself severely reprimanded, etc.!
Mary I know it looks bad, Headmaster.
Tom Looks bad?
Mary But I did it in all good faith for those three kids!
Tom I know you did, I know where you're coming from, but good grief, there are five hundred students in this school with exactly the same kind of outlook as your three musketeers!
Mary I know that.
Tom How many trips to London would it take to get them all there? I'm not saying it was wrong educationally! Good grief, if we had the resources I'd take the whole lot of them. Well, maybe not the whole school, but you know what I'm saying.
Mary The way I see it is, these kids haven't got a chance and if I can help raise their expectations, just ever so slightly, then that's what I'll do. Now I'm sorry that it might not suit, and I'm sorry that they might get caught nicking mincemeat, but as long as I'm here, which is not for much longer, I'm going to keep at it! Because if I don't, I might as well be some other members of staff here, and look forward to two weeks in France and threaten to write a bloody campus novel!
Tom Now, I don't think there's any need to get personal!
Mary Teaching is personal, Tom! If you went in a classroom more often you'd see that. I thought things were supposed to have changed? If you ask me it's exactly as it was fifteen years ago! It's worse if anything! It's all about teachers in a classroom with kids. It's about relationships.
Tom Well, I have to tell you that I have been in teaching all my life and I have never been spoken to like this.
Mary Well, there you go, like I said, there's a first time for everything!

Music. The Lights fade

SCENE 3

Drama studio

Stacey, Kerry and Maggie enter

They are practising for their dance piece to music from the ghetto blaster. (Any disco music with a strong beat could be used.) We see from the work that the piece is based on freedom and oppression, it has many closed down and opening out gestures. The girls are getting good, but it is still quite raw. We don't see any movement that we would in any way describe as impressive. Mary switches off the ghetto blaster and the girls get their breath back

Mary That's a lot b-better, but it's still not right. We've had three weeks stuck at this level, what's happening? If you want to get through the heats you'll have to work harder than that! You'll have to concentrate more, Maggie! Remember the crispness of the movement, remember what we saw in London?

Maggie I'll never forget it, that Ronny tried to get in our room.

Mary That's your problem, you can't concentrate for longer than a minute. Just think about it. What are we after? What did the dance have?

Stacey Attitude!

Mary Well, you've got attitude!

Kerry Attack!

Mary All the m-movements had an edge!

Stacey We can't get that, can we?

Mary Why not? We're as good as them, aren't we?

Maggie I can't get sharp, I can get blunt, but can I hellers like get sharp!

Stacey Shall we do it again?

Maggie I'm knackered! I can't get my breath.

Mary And you need to cut the fags!

Maggie I would, but they're the only things that keep me going!

Stacey Come on, we've only got until next weekend, you snot!

Maggie Bog!

Kerry Miss, can't we do it every day?

Maggie Yes, Miss, If you got me out of Science, I'd blossom, I know I would!

Jimmy enters

Jimmy Right, Pan's People, are we ready?

Mary You've just missed them!

Jimmy Are they getting any better or what?

Mary Not bad!

Kerry I thought we were brilliant!
Jimmy Are we ready, then I can drop you off!
Maggie Ace, I'm knackered!

Mary collects the ghetto blaster and begins tidying up

Mary OK, let's call that it for tonight! Same again on Thursday! Is that all
    right, Kerry, can you manage Thursday?
Kerry Don't know, miss.
Maggie Miss, don't forget to try and get us out of all the other lessons.
Mary How's your grandma?
Kerry It's not looking good, miss, and now the dog's bad!
Mary Oh dear!

Mary exits with the ghetto blaster

*Jimmy offers the keys to Maggie. The girls collect their bags and tracksuits
and drift away. Jimmy hangs about, so does Stacey*

Jimmy Here's the keys if you want to go and get in the bus.
Maggie It's dangerous leaving it around here, didn't you know that?
Jimmy Well, there's nothing to nick, is there?
Kerry Except the bus! Mind you, it can't be worth more than fifty quid!

Maggie and Kerry exit

Stacey and Jimmy are together

Jimmy Is it going all right, then?
Stacey Yes!
Jimmy Enjoying it?
Stacey Yes!
Jimmy You're putting the hours in, aren't you?
Stacey You've got to, haven't you?

A beat

Jimmy I'm pleased.
Stacey Eh?
Jimmy I'm pleased!
Stacey I bet you hate it.
Jimmy I don't know, I think I'm developing a taste for it.
Stacey It's a bit raunchy!

Jimmy I thought it might be!

Stacey It's a bit modern, Dad. A bit Britney Spears.

Jimmy Well, I liked that one.

Stacey I thought you hated her video?

Jimmy I say all sorts, you ought to know me by now!

Stacey So are we off, then?

Jimmy I just want to have a word with Mrs Clifford.

Stacey Oh, right.

Jimmy Well, anyway!

Stacey You've gone all red!

Jimmy It's just warm in here, that's all.

A beat

Stacey I'll wait in the bus, then.

Stacey exits as Mary enters

Jimmy I, er…

Mary What?

Jimmy Well…?

Mary It's funny because…

Jimmy What…?

Mary Well, I was out of order in London.

Jimmy Oh, that?

Mary Anyway, I'd better…

Jimmy Let you go…

Mary OK, nice to…

Jimmy I was just thinking…

Mary What?

Jimmy Do you like Indian food?

Mary Sorry?

Jimmy Do you like curries?

Mary Me?

Jimmy I just wondered…

Mary …W-well…

Jimmy I mean, if you don't…

Mary …Well, actually…

Jimmy …Because there's a very good curry house near where we live and…

Mary Oh, right.

Jimmy I mean, if you're not…

Mary Indian?

Jimmy It was just a thought.

Mary Oh, right…
Jimmy But if you're not interested. We can leave it!
Mary Oh, right…
Jimmy Anyway!

Jimmy exits

Mary continues to collect her school things

Tom enters, he is completely under stress and looks awful

Tom Oh, I thought I was the only one left!
Mary Just going…
Tom Sometimes I walk through the school when everyone's gone. Funny feeling, all those empty classrooms, all those lives we've helped…
Mary Or not!

A beat

Tom I suppose this term has gone quite quickly for you?
Mary In some respects!
Tom Well, we've been pleased to have you. Any plans?
Mary Not at the moment!
Tom So the adjudicators are coming here, are they?
Mary I thought it would be a good idea to invite them. They came to have a look and liked it. There are about ten schools taking part. I spoke to the Chairman of the…
Tom Yes, yes, she said.
Mary I hope you don't mind…
Tom Well, I would have preferred it if you'd have mentioned it!
Mary Well, I would have done but you always seemed to be up to your neck.

Silence

Tom Has anyone mentioned this to the local press?
Mary Not as far as I…
Tom Well, you'd better leave that with me. We've got to let the outside world know what we are up to, you know, Mrs Clifford. We can't hide our talents under a bushel, etc. It's a shop window, etc. What if we win, etc. Good grief think about the coverage? Anyway, fingers crossed. Foxy's basketball team are through to the semis, and now this! Very good! If it wasn't for the Science department fire, I'd have cause for cautious optimism! (*He turns to depart, then stops*) Not a bad old school, is it?

Mary No, not at all!
Tom Especially when all the kids have gone. I jest of course!

Tom exits

Music. Black-out

SCENE 4

Indian restaurant. Night

Music

An Indian-style dance piece brings on a small table, set with Indian food

Mary and Jimmy sit at the table. Mary is tucking into the wine but hasn't touched much food. Jimmy plays with a chapati

Jimmy You know the first time I had a curry, I wondered what chapatis were. I thought they were towels, I wiped my mouth on two of them, you should have seen Cheryl's face. She thought I was an animal! You don't seem to have eaten much.
Mary Well, Indian isn't my...
Jimmy Well, why didn't you say?
Mary I was b-being polite. I thought it must have taken you ages to pluck up the courage to ask me and I didn't want to offend you.
Jimmy You wouldn't have offended me, I always come here on a Wednesday.
Mary Oh, right! (*She drinks another glass of plonk*)
Jimmy I'll have yours if you don't want it.
Mary Do you mind if I just pick at it, it's helping the wine.
Jimmy Is it good, it's the best they had?
Mary Well...
Jimmy Nearly four quid a bottle. I mean I don't know wine, but...
Mary After the first three glasses I'll drink anything, so...
Jimmy You could have had a pint.
Mary No, this is fine. I needed my teeth cleaning anyway! It's taken the first layer of enamel off already!
Jimmy I always have a lager!
Mary I've always been unlucky with wine! I don't know which colour you should have with fish or meat or any of that!

Silence

Peter used to ask friends from college around, and I never knew what to
give them!
Jimmy Who's Peter?
Mary My husband. My ex-husband.
Jimmy Oh, right.

Silence. Mary has another drink

Mary It's not bad wine actually!

A beat

Jimmy What is it that they say about teachers? Those who can't teach, and
those who can't … what is it?
Mary Those who can, do, those who can't, teach, and those who can't teach,
teach PE.
Jimmy That's right.
Mary And those who can't teach PE teach other teachers to teach PE!
Jimmy Ay, I knew it was something like that.
Mary Take no notice of that bollocks. A good teacher can take a kid's life
and phooogh, magic!
Jimmy You believe that shite, do you?
Mary That's what happened to me. I had this one teacher who took us to see
Death of a Salesman. I thought, that's my dad on stage, except that he
wasn't American, and he wasn't called Willy and he wasn't a salesman, he
was called Keith and he worked on the buses. B-But it didn't matter, it was
like a light had gone on in my head! (*She knocks back another glass of
wine*)

Silence

So what about you, then?
Jimmy Me?
Mary What's happened to Mrs Naylor?
Jimmy Well…
Mary You don't have to tell me.
Jimmy She … er … died.
Mary Oh.
Jimmy Three years ago!

Silence

Mary Oh, I'm sorry.

Jimmy Aneurysm!
Mary I'm sorry for asking.

A beat

Jimmy That's when Stacey went to stay with her aunt in Hammersmith. We
   didn't speak! I don't know… I didn't know what to say.

A beat

Mary Language lets us down on those occasions, don't you think? Beckett
   and Joyce hardly ever used words at all when they spent time together!
   Anyway! (*She has another drink*)

A very long silence

Jimmy I'm sorry.
Mary What for?
Jimmy This is a mistake.
Mary What is?
Jimmy I shouldn't have invited you!
Mary Don't worry, it's f-f-fine. I shouldn't have…
Jimmy I've got nothing to say! I've got nothing to talk about?
Mary Of course you have.
Jimmy I thought we had a lot in common, but we haven't. I mean I could
   write my life story on the back of a beer mat.
Mary You're not thick, though, are you?
Jimmy Aren't I?
Mary I don't think you are!
Jimmy I bloody am, and as far as I can remember I have been all my bloody
   life!

*Music. Jimmy sings. Mary sits and listens and continues to drink and pick at
her food. The Lights change*

Song 7: I Remember When

Jimmy   Jimmy Naylor five years old
                   Now be good at school that's what I'm told
                   I hated school in every way
                   I was happy when I missed a day.

                   And at the age of ten
                   I ran to school and back again

My teacher's like this big fat hen.
Oh, I remember when…

Yes, I remember when…
Yes, I remember when…
Yes, I remember…

When in my fourteenth year
Moustache, muscles, all the latest gear
You stopping on at school?
Who me? No fear!
I needed women, song and beer!

At seventeen I knew it all
And at the Brewers Arms I'd call
Then vomit ill against a wall.
Oh, I remember when…

Yes, I remember when…
Yes, I remember when…
Yes, I remember…

On my wedding day?
Bride in white so bright and gay
My whole life was changed that day.
I loved her in every way…

Girls   Do you remember when

Girls Jimmy now you're twenty-four,	**Jimmy** Jimmy Naylor twenty-four,
With a little girl, expecting more	A little girl, expecting more
There's unsettled bills and debts galore	Unsettled bills and debts galore
Do you	All through my life I've wanted
Do you remember	more.
Yes, I remember when…	Yes, I remember when…
I just listen to my heart and then	Yes, I remember when…
Yes, I remember…	Yes, I …
Doo doo doo doo doo doo doo	When I was twenty-nine
Doo doo doo he was doing	Three years I'd been doing time
He was doing time	
Doo doo doo though he'd lost the plot	And though I'd lost the plot
He felt he was doing	I was doing fine…
He was he was doing fine	Yes, I was doing

Instrumental/dance break

Stacey   I just think about the past and then
               How I remember ...
               Remember when

Jimmy   Jimmy Naylor thirty-eight
               Full of bitterness and hate
               My search for meaning came a little too late
               Is this to be my fate?

Girls Ooh ooh whoo-oo   **Jimmy** Can you remember when?
          Whoa-oa whoa oh-oh ho   You were five and you were ten
Girls   Whoa-whoa whoa
                 Yeah
                                            Jimmy What were you doing then?
Girls   Can you remember?
                 Can you remember?
                 Can you remember?
Girls Can you remember?   **Jimmy** Can you remember?
          When?   When?

Music ends. Mary and Jimmy resume their dinner date

Mary So what do you fancy doing?
Jimmy Eh?
Mary Shall we split the bill?
Jimmy I think we'd better, I've no cash on me.
Mary So what have you got on you?
Jimmy Nothing.
Mary What?
Jimmy Nothing.
Mary Well, thank you!
Jimmy That's what I'm saying. I should never have asked you. My mouth
          runs away with me. As soon as I asked you to come, I realized I hadn't got
          any spare cash.
Mary What are you like?
Jimmy I mean, I've got a cheque book, but it'll probably bounce all over the
          bloody restaurant.
Mary Well, it's been a nice evening, I've come for a meal I don't like, I've
          drunk dreadful wine and now I'm going to pay for it. You really know how
          to give a woman a good time, don't you?
Jimmy Sorry!
Mary How was yours by the way?
Jimmy Mine was absolutely excellent.
Mary Oh, that's good, I'm pl-pleased you enjoyed it!

Jimmy Mine was fine!

Mary So what do you fancy? A disco and carriages at dawn?

Jimmy A disco? Are you joking?

Mary The night is still young. Besides, I'm leaving Common Road at the end of the month so why not?

Jimmy A disco. Bloody hell? I haven't been to one for years!

Mary Neither have I, so you must let me treat you.

Jimmy Are you serious?

Mary Well, we'll not get another drink in here, will we? I think the head waiter went home at half ten. Down to a club, then, shall we? There must be an over thirty-fives night somewhere!

Jimmy Woman, you're a bloody liability.

Mary Oh, shut up, you bo-boring sod, and live a bit. Now where's that bit of plastic? (*She shouts*) Waiter!

Disco music plays

Black-out

SCENE 5

Disco. Night

Music. Mirror ball

The three girls strike the restaurant set, and we are in a disco, clubbing to seventies-style music. Routine very sub seventies with the girls at the back dressed in seventies gear doing seventies routines

SCENE 6

Marina. Night

Music fades. The Lights change

Mary and Jimmy walk slowly DS. *Mary is stuffing a kebab in her face. Jimmy breathes in the night air. They are trying to sober up*

Mary Oh, look at me!

Jimmy Eh?

Mary I said look at me. I'm educated to the p-point of the ridiculous and I'm still capable of making an arsehole of myself.

Jimmy Now that's a skill!

Mary Yes, it is. That is a real skill, and ought to be regarded as such!

Jimmy Not a bad club, was it?

Mary I thought you said you could bloody dance?

Jimmy I thought I could.

Mary Well, you couldn't dance in there, could you? I thought you were having a fit!

Jimmy Hey, I taught St Vitus how to dance, did you know that?

Mary Very good!

Jimmy Yes! St Vitus dance, hey, not bad!

Mary (*with a Scottish accent*) Very good, Jimmy, I saw it coming a mile off, mate!

A beat

Jimmy You know, I don't drink usually. I gave all that up a long time ago.

Mary Well, you obviously need some therapy for that!

Jimmy Yes, that was another avenue of pleasure that I decided to close down.

Mary They never change, do they, kebabs? They are always the same, it's like one of the few things in the world that you can actually rely on. A kebab is a metaphor for how you feel at the end of an evening, isn't it? All scabby and falling to bits!

Jimmy I mean, look at us, what are we doing? It's a quarter to three!

Mary Well, I've got nothing to rush home for!

Jimmy No.

Mary No.

A beat

Jimmy You're a bad influence!

Mary Am I?

Jimmy Yes.

Mary Good!

A beat

Jimmy I was thinking the other day, you know?

Mary Oh dear!

Jimmy I know, outrageous.

Mary A very bad sign!

Jimmy Oh ay, I got thinking.

Mary Nice kebab actually!

Jimmy Do you know what about?
Mary Could have done with a bit more sauce, but…
Jimmy Art.
Mary Oh, shit!
Jimmy That's what I thought.
Mary Bloody fattening these, though…
Jimmy You know what I thought? If you asked ordinary people…
Mary You're not bloody ordinary, are you? You're anything but ordinary. Ordinary people don't take kids to brothels, or go marching into schools demanding their kids back!
Jimmy They do, that's where you're wrong, that's exactly what ordinary people do!
Mary There is no such thing as an ordinary person, anyway!
Jimmy Shut up a minute! Who asked you anyway? Right, if you asked ordinary people if they thought art was important they'd probably say no, you know, unless they thought about it, they'd probably give a pat answer.
Mary Probably!
Jimmy And yet, everybody has pictures up! Bloody hypocrites, eh? I don't know any houses that don't have pictures on the walls.
Mary Yes, but the same people don't gives a toss when they close galleries or theatres because they think it doesn't affect them!
Jimmy I can see that, that's what I could see. Bloody hypocrites.
Mary It's too much effort for them. "The ordinary people will sell their liberty for a quiet life!" Anthony Burgess!
Jimmy Even when I was in the nick, I put a bloody picture up. It was a photo of me and Stace, Cheryl took it at Lowestoft!
Mary Yes, if they could see me now. Oh, yes, if only, what would my mother say? She spent half her life trying to stop me going to discos and eating kebabs. And here I am!

A beat. Mary belches loudly. Jimmy laughs

Jimmy What would it be like if all the bloody teachers were like you?
Mary They should all be like me. Then we'd have a decent education system!
Jimmy That's right!
Mary A world class system! We'd have teachers in schools that were that alive, and committed, that bloody interesting and human that they'd frighten the kids out of their stupor!

A beat

I feel a bit sick to be honest, I think I might have eaten that kebab a bit too quick!

A beat

Jimmy Oh hell, you're a mad woman!

Silence

Mary So then?
Jimmy What?
Mary What happens next?
Jimmy What?
Mary What happens after this…?

Music starts

Song 8: What Next

Jimmy   We could stand and freeze,
                   Have another kebab.
                   And in a moment or two, I could call you a cab.
Mary   I should really go home.

Jimmy   What, home to the gloom?
                   Home to your books?
                   Home to the cold, and sat all by yourself in your room?
Mary   I'm getting too old for this

Jimmy   Too old for what?
                   Wasn't it you who said,
                   This was the only chance that we got?
Mary   Why spoil a good night?

Jimmy   It's not over yet!
                   I've just woken up to the fact,
                   You're the funniest woman I've met!
Mary   Do you think we should kiss?

Jimmy   Now you're going all shy,
                   If tonight is the night,
                   Then we both ought to give it a try.
Mary   But what if it's lust?

Jimmy   Who cares what it is?
                   Let's just jump in a cab
                   and get right down to the biz!

Mary   But what after that?
               Think how we'll feel.

Jimmy   We've had a dream of a night! Haven't we?
               And suddenly you're getting all real!
Mary   In the morning I'll leave,
               Sneak out through the door.
               I'll regret all the things that we've done
Mary & Jimmy Like I've been here before.
               Never learnt through the years
               Never learnt through the pain
               Never learnt through the times that I said
               I'd never do this thing again!
Jimmy   But do you think we should kiss?

Mary   Will it last beyond this?
Jimmy   We could stand and freeze
               Have another kebab
               In a minute or two I could call you a cab!
Mary & Jimmy But do you think?
               Do you think?
               But do you think … we should…?

They kiss. Black-out

SCENE 7

Drama studio

*Maggie, Stacey and Kerry rush on stage. They have just completed their
piece in the heats of the dance competition, they are very excitable but with
a tinge of dissappointment*

Maggie It's over, thank God, I was shitting myself up there!
Kerry Yeah, we know that!
Maggie And I thought I was going to spew!
Kerry Why did you have to cock it up?
Maggie I thought I was going to heave my guts up, that's why. Anyway, it
    weren't me, it was Stace!
Stacey Bog!
Maggie Snot!
Stacey Mag, you were three bloody steps out!

Kerry She can't count, that's why!

Maggie Bog!

Stacey We looked crap! Absolute shite!

Maggie Nobody probably even noticed.

Stacey Well, they'd have to be blind, wouldn't they, we went left and you went chuffin' right!

Maggie Bog!

Stacey Snot!

Kerry I'm glad we were last, though, are you? It meant we could watch all the others. They were good from Grimsby, weren't they?

Stacey They were better than us, we looked like spastics 'cos of her!

Maggie Was that the one about the end of the world?

Kerry I thought it was good.

Maggie I thought it was a bit too obvious!

Stacey What do you know?

Kerry Do you think the judge understood ours?

Maggie I don't see why he should, I didn't and I'm in it!

Mary enters, she is delighted with them

Mary What are you doing in here?

Maggie Gagging for a fag!

Stacey Miss, we were shit, weren't we?

Maggie Miss, I thought I was going to chuck up. It all came into my throat.

Stacey How long does it take them to decide, miss?

Mary It might take an hour, or if they all agree it may just take a few minutes!

Stacey We've not won, no way, we were rubbish!

Mary Well, listen, if you haven't, keep it together, all right? Remember what we said. No big emotions, no histrionics, it's all about control, OK?

Jimmy enters

They groan

Stacey So what do you think?

Jimmy Not bad.

Another groan

Stacey We were crap!

Jimmy A few steps out, but...

Mary Just ignore him, let's go and see what the judges have got to say...

Jimmy They've done that!

Maggie And?
Stacey We're not through, are we?

A beat

Jimmy It doesn't look like it!

Silence

Maggie What?

A beat

Jimmy Not by the looks of it!
Mary They must have got something. A recommendation, or a commendation, or something?
Jimmy Not according to what they've just said. A school from Beverley's won it.

Silence

Maggie Well, fuck me!
Mary That's quite enough of that! Thank you, we can use language much smarter than that, Margaret Brooke!
Maggie Piss off, you silly gett!
Mary Thank you!
Maggie Piss off, all of you…
Mary Maggie…?

Music

Song 9: Not Worth It!

Maggie   You were the one who built us up!
                  You were the one who gave us hope.
                  You were the one who said we'd fly
                  Reach for the sky
                  And never cry.
                  And now you see that we can't cope!

                  You were the one who gave us faith
                  You found us food so we would grow.
                  But to me it was all crap

It was all false,
A bad mishap!
It was bullshit and that you know!

You were the one with big ideas
You made us trust you and believe
You worked us hard, you made us sweat
And now we're scarred.
You must think we're so naïve?

And nothing that you say or do.

All   Will change the way I feel for you.
I hate your hopes and all your dreams

Maggie   I hate your methods,
And your means
I hate the pain you've put us through

You should have known that we'd be shit,
Not worth the effort, yeah, that's it!
No self-esteem
Not worth the fuss
No, not anyone of us!
We're just the pits,
The detritus!

Kerry & Stacey (*overlapping Maggie*) We're not worth it
Not worth it
We're not worth it
Not worth it

Maggie   You should have known that we'd be shit
Not worth the effort, is that it?
No self-esteem
Not worth the fuss.

But did you do it just for us?
Did you do it just for us?
Did you do it just for us?

Or for yourself to get a buzz?
And now you're finished…!
…Just like us!
Well now you're finished
Just like us!

Maggie, Kerry and Stacey depart in tears

Jimmy Mind you, I thought it was a bit shoddy, myself!
Mary What?
Jimmy I was just saying, I thought some of it was all over the place. I mean compared to what we saw in London I thought it looked slack. Well, it's only my opinion, but it seemed to lack any edge.
Mary Just shut up!
Jimmy I've got an opinion.
Mary Well, keep them to yourself.
Jimmy I mean, I was bored to death watching them all, so I'm entitled to a bloody opinion!
Mary Why don't you just shut up?
Jimmy I'm only expressing an opinion!
Mary They did really well.
Jimmy They did all right, but for me what's the point in doing it if you don't win. You can say they all had a great experience but…
Mary Oh, shut up, you silly man!

A beat

Jimmy Is what I am, is it?
Mary Yes, that's what you are!

A beat

Jimmy Not good enough, is that it?
Mary No.
Jimmy A mistake, was it?
Mary Like you said!

A beat

Jimmy Well, anyway.
Mary It was a good night.
Jimmy It was an excellent night.
Mary I thought it was what I needed. But…
Jimmy What about me? What about if it's what I need?
Mary Don't.
Jimmy What if that's what it's about?

Music. The Lights change

   Mary and Jimmy look at each other, then they exit

Song 10: Remember When

Jimmy appears lit by a spotlight

We hear the intro of the song and catch the chorus

Jimmy   Jimmy Naylor forty-four
                   Always knew that there was more.
                   What am I looking for?
                   What am I looking for?
                   Oh, I remember when...
                   Yes, I remember when
                   Yes, I remember...

Jimmy exits

The Lights fade

SCENE 8

Main hall. A month later

Music

We are in the main hall of the school, the audience become the large school assembly

Stacey and Maggie dressed in track suits are setting up chairs on stage

Tom enters. He is dressed extra smart and wears an emblem for cancer care on his lapel. He places his papers on stage. He has developed a slight stammer as part of a stressful nervous tick

Mary enters. She too looks extra smart

Tom M-morning!
Mary Morning.
Tom I always find it a curiously emotional day; the last assembly for Year Eleven! I've w-wanted to get rid of them for a year and now they're actually off into the big grey yonder, I wonder how they'll get along!
Mary I think they're survivors, Tom.
Tom Survive doing what, though, that's my worry.
Mary Like you said, you can only do so much!
Tom Have you got a moment, Mrs Clifford?

Mary Well, I think so.

Tom Could I have an unofficial word?

Mary If you like!

Tom I don't know if you're aware, but, but, but we've still been unable to appoint a replacement for Ron Baker.

Mary Well, I had heard something…

Tom And the Chair has asked me to ask you, why you hadn't applied?

Mary Well, I hadn't applied, Tom, because the arts are given such a low priority in this school.

Tom Yes, yes, yes!

Mary There didn't seem to be any point.

Tom Yes, yes, I see.

Mary The job is a hiding for nothing as far as I'm concerned.

Tom Oh, no, no, no!

Mary And I didn't want to outstay my welcome.

Tom Oh, no, don't worry about that.

Mary Besides, it's knackering…

Tom Yes, it is. It must be.

Mary …just getting the kids around here to respond to anything…

Tom Yes, yes, yes!

Mary And anyway, the arts can't really be quantified, can they, Tom?

Tom Well, that seems unfair!

Mary Well, that's me, you see, Tom, I think life is unfair. And as it's my last day, I suppose I can say what I like!

Tom Yes, yes, yes, I can appreciate that!

Mary Did you see the dance piece?

Tom No, I was at the basketball.

Mary Lost, didn't they?

Tom Trounced sadly, Foxy was gutted.

Mary Yes, I bet he was.

Tom The Chairman saw it and was very…

Mary Funny thing about the arts, I was thinking this the other day. What's so special about them? Well, they make you use your imagination, and of course without a developed imagination how can we expect anyone to think?

Tom Yes, yes, good point!

Mary And they make you feel. It's as simple as that. They make you feel, Tom!

Mary turns to sit down

Tom Since we're talking about the job I wondered if you might want to drop your application into my office, Mrs Clifford.

Mary I'll think about it, Tom.

Tom And actually, since we're still in our official capacities, I wonder, could you refer to me as Headmaster, Mrs Clifford?

Mary Well, actually, since we are still in our official capacities could you refer to me as Dr Clifford, Headmaster?

Tom Oh, yes, yes, no trouble at all. I assume you'll be applying for the job in that case, Doctor?

Mary If you assume you make an ass of you and me, Tom!

It is now time for Tom to address the school

I think you are nearly on, Tom.

Tom I'll just grab my notes, Doctor!

Tom exits

Jimmy comes on stage. He is dressed in smartish clothes, and is carrying a bunch of flowers

Jimmy I just wanted to say thanks.

Mary I don't want a scene!

Jimmy I just think what you've done for Stacey and the others is great.

Mary I only switched the light on!

Jimmy Well, whatever.

A beat

Mary You needn't have … the flowers.

Jimmy Oh, these, these are for Stacey!

Mary Oh, that's nice!

A beat

Jimmy Well, that's what you do, isn't it?

Tom enters and goes to the front of the stage

Mary You better sit down!

Tom addresses the audience

Tom Well, welcome! Welcome. It's nice to see so many old faces here today, and I'd like to thank those parents who've come to support us. We live in difficult times. And it is very rewarding to be able to tell you about some of the successes of our young people. We have a full and varied programme of events for you. Now many of you will know already that Common Road

High has always been a keen supporter of the arts. Where would we be without them? We recognize that they are a crucial and fundamental development tool for our young people! I was thinking only the other day. What's so special about the arts? Two things came into my mind. They make us use our imaginations, and where would we be without an imagination? Unable to think, bereft of fantasy, unable to live in a conceptual universe! And secondly they make us feel, they make us feel human. Now we are especially lucky to have such a highly qualified teacher as Mrs Dr Clifford, Dr Mrs Clifford, working with us! Now, I'd like to introduce a trio of girls, who have been working very hard over the last two terms on a new development in school. Modern Dance! Now Stacey, Maggie and Kelly entered a national dance competition and although they didn't win, they showed a high level of determination, and they wanted to show their piece to the rest of Year Eleven before they left! You never know, we might just see them on Top of the Pops one day! I jest, of course but... So come on, Kelly, Maggie and Stacey! (*He returns to his seat*)

Stacey, Kerry and Maggie walk shyly on stage. They bring a large ghetto-blaster with them

Kerry Kerry!

Stacey This is the dance that we did with Mrs Clifford. And though we didn't think it at the time, winning isn't everything!

Kerry No, but it's nice.

Stacey Yes, it's nice, but it isn't everything!

Maggie And I'd like to say, that we'd like to do some more dance, miss...

Kerry If you're interested.

Stacey But if you're not, well...

Maggie Sod you, then!

Kerry You thick gett!

Maggie So what?

Silence

Stacey Well, anyway! This is it. Oh, by the way. Karl Evans! I think you're brilliant!

Maggie Oh God...

Kerry Get on with it.

Stacey clicks on the ghetto-blaster. Loud music emits from the machine. The trio embark on a very stylized and highly energetic closely synchronized dance. Which involves fast foot movements, drops, expansions and energetic kicks. It finishes with a flourish. The girls are breathless and tired at the end of it

Tom stands from his seat and applauds. Jimmy is nearby. Mary applauds and makes her way down to meet the girls who are exhausted

Tom Well done, girls, that was smashing!
Jimmy Smashing? It was bloody excellent, man!
Tom Yes, yes, it was excellent, well done! Well done!

The girls are on their knees

Maggie Oh, hell, I'm going to spew!
Stacey Yes, I think I am!
Kerry I'm shaking like a leaf, me!
Maggie Ohhh…
Stacey (*with love*) Not bad, you snot!
Maggie What?
Stacey I said, "Not bad!"
Maggie Bog!
Stacey Oh, leave it!

Mary comes DS *to the girls*

Mary Well, what can I say?
Maggie Miss, I'm shagged.
Stacey Miss, I am.
Kerry So was it any good, miss?
Mary What can I say?

Music

Song 11: Not Worth It

Maggie   You were the one who built us up,
              You were the one who gave us hope.
              You were the one who said we'd fly
              Reach for the sky,
              And never cry.
              And now we see that you can't cope!

Kerry   You were the one who gave us faith,
              You found us food so we would grow.
              But to me it was all crap,
              It was all false,
              A bad mishap.
              I guess we really didn't know!

To the audience

Stacey   And you all thought that we'd be shit.
                Not worth the effort, is that it?
                No self-esteem
                Not worth the fuss
                No, not any one of us.
                We're not the pits.
                The detritus!

Maggie   'Cos we are worth it!
Maggie & Kerry We are worth it!
All Girls   We are worth it!
                We're worth it.
Stacey   We are worth it!

All Girls   We are worth it!
                We are worth it!
                We are worth it!
                We're worth it!

                And you all thought that we'd be shit.
                Not worth the effort, is that it?
                No self-esteem,
                Not worth the fuss
                Is that what you think of us?

Tom & Jimmy & Mary (*overlapping the girls*) They are worth it!
                They are worth it!
                They are worth it!
                They are worth it!
All Girls   Is that what you think of us.
                We're worth it!
                We're worth it
                We're worth it.

Stacey   We are worth it!

*The girls sing, and raise their hands. Backing support fills the stage. The girls
are triumphant*

Black-out

CURTAIN

FURNITURE AND PROPERTY LIST

Further dressing may be added at the director's discretion

ACT I

SCENE 1

On stage: Chairs (to be set and re-set throughout)

Off stage: Note cards (**Tom**)
Papers (**All**)
Files, books, basketball (**Gary**)

Personal: **Mary**: glasses (worn throughout)

SCENE 2

Personal: **Maggie**: headphones

SCENE 3

Off stage: Briefcase containing papers (**Mary**)
Bags (**Stacey**)

SCENE 4

Off stage: Books, papers (**Tom**)

Personal: **Tom**: car keys
Mary: mobile phone

SCENE 5

On stage: As before

SCENE 6

On stage: As before

SCENE 7

On stage: Can of beer

SCENE 8

Off stage: Files, papers (**Tom**)

SCENE 9

Off stage: Rucksacks, suitcases (**Girls**)
Holdall, steering wheel (**Jimmy**)

ACT II

SCENE 1

On stage: Chairs (to be set and re-set throughout)

Off stage: Baggage (**Girls & Mary**)
Bags (**Jimmy**)
2 glasses of brandy (**Ronnie**)

Personal: **Mary:** scarf
Ronnie: glasses with an eye blacked out
Maggie: call girl cards
Jimmy: lighter, cigarette

SCENE 2

On stage: As before

SCENE 3

On stage: Ghetto-blaster
School things

Off stage: Keys (**Jimmy**)
Bags, tracksuits (**Girls**)

SCENE 4

Off stage: Small table, set with Indian food, wine, chapati (**Stage Management**)

SCENE 5

On stage: Mirror ball

SCENE 6

Off stage: Kebab (**Mary**)

SCENE 7

On stage: As before

SCENE 8

On stage: Chairs

Off stage: Papers (**Tom**)
              Bunch of flowers (**Jimmy**)
              Large ghetto blaster (**Stacey** & **Kerry** & **Maggie**)

Personal: **Tom:** emblem for cancer care

LIGHTING PLOT

Property fittings required: nil
Various interiors and exteriors

ACT I, Prologue

To open: Black-out

Cue 1 **Actors** speak   (Page 1)
Vertical spotlight on each until all five are lit

ACT I, Scene 1

To open: Morning

Cue 2 **Mary**: "…in the f-f-first place!"   (Page 6)
Fade lights

ACT I, Scene 2

To open: General lighting

Cue 3 **Girls** start to move to the music   (Page 12)
Change lights

Cue 4 Music stops   (Page 14)
Return to previous state

ACT I, Scene 3

To open: Night lighting

Cue 5 **Mary**: "At home?"   (Page 19)
Change lights for song

Cue 6   Musical refrain   (Page 20)
               Fade lights to black-out

ACT I, Scene 4

To open: Night lighting

No cues

ACT I, Scene 5

To open: Rippling water effects

Cue 7   **Jimmy** exits   (Page 24)
               Fade lights to black-out

ACT I, Scene 6

To open: Overall general lighting

Cue 8   Music plays   (Page 27)
               Black-out

ACT I, Scene 7

To open: Overall general lighting

Cue 9   **Jimmy** and **Stacey** look at each other   (Page 30)
               Fade lights

ACT I, Scene 8

To open: Overall general lighting

Cue 10   Music plays   (Page 34)
               Fade lights

ACT I, SCENE 9

To open: Overall general lighting

Cue 11   **All**: "Break away!"   (Page 40)
            Black-out

ACT II, PROLOGUE

To open: Darkness

Cue 12   Music gets louder and louder   (Page 41)
            Spotlight on **Girls**, *and separately on* **Mary**; *sequence*
              of flashing lights

Cue 13   Tiredness sets in   (Page 41)
            Fade lights to Black-out

ACT II, SCENE 1

To open: Overall general lighting

Cue 14   **Girls** exit   (Page 55)
            Change lights

Cue 15   **Jimmy** and **Mary** exit   (Page 55)
            Fade lights to Black-out

ACT II, SCENE 2

To open: Strong spotlight on **Tom**

Cue 16   Music plays   (Page 57)
            Fade lights

ACT II, SCENE 3

To open: Overall general lighting

Cue 17   Music plays   (Page 62)
            Black-out

ACT II, Scene 4

To open: Restaurant lighting

Cue 18   **Jimmy** sings and **Mary** listens   (Page 64)
            Change lights

Cue 19   Disco music plays   (Page 67)
            Black-out

ACT II, Scene 5

To open: Mirror ball effects

No cues

ACT II, Scene 6

To open: Marina night lighting

Cue 20   **Jimmy** and **Mary** kiss   (Page 71)
            Black-out

ACT II, Scene 7

To open: Overall general lighting

Cue 21   **Jimmy** enters   (Page 72)
            Spotlight on **Jimmy**

Cue 22   **Jimmy** exits   (Page 76)
            Fade lights

ACT II, Scene 8

To open: Overall general lighting

Cue 23   **Girls** are triumphant   (Page 81)
            Black-out

EFFECTS PLOT

ACT I

ACT II

COPYRIGHT MUSIC